the horsemen

the horsemen

Jack Engelhard

HENRY REGNERY COMPANY—CHICAGO

Library of Congress Cataloging in Publication Data

Engelhard, Jack.
The horsemen.

1. Horsemen. 2. Blum, Walter, 1934 or 5-
3. Horse-racing. I. Title.
SF336.A2E53 797'.43'0922 (B) 74-6889
ISBN 0-8092-8399-9

In appreciation to David Appel

Published by Henry Regnery Company
114 West Illinois Street, Chicago, Illinois 60610
Manufactured in the United States of America
Library of Congress Catalog Card Number: 74-6889
International Standard Book Number: 0-8092-8399-9

To Leslie

Wednesday Morning

Chapter 1

The summer of 1973 was an especially sunny season for thoroughbred racing. A year before the sport had been suffering through some dark days, writhing under the cloud of a House Select Committee on Crime, which was holding public hearings on the claims of an admitted racketeer who asserted that doped horses and fixed races were the rule rather than the exception. Although the charges were never substantiated, and even though racing's own watchdog, the Thoroughbred Racing Protective Bureau, had been the agency that apprehended "Mr. X" and his confreres as one example of racing's ability to clean its own house, thoroughbred racing was regarded with heightened suspicion by a public that always, regardless of public hearings, had its doubts about the Sport of Kings, despite the fact that at the time the integrity even of "human" athletes and athletics was being prominently questioned in regard to betting, fixing, and drugs.

Then in early 1973, like a terminal patient who suddenly finds the doctor with the miracle cure, racing recovered, drew open the blinds, and saw the sun. The antidote was Secretariat, the first thoroughbred to win the Triple Crown in twenty-five years, culminating the sweep with a devastating thirty-one-length victory in the Belmont. Secretariat, the big red machine, the super horse, would make the cover of *Time*, would be named *Sport* magazine's Man of the Year, and would become a star of television. On his powerful shoulders he lifted racing back to its glory, while his owner, Penny Tweedy, seen on television as articulate, gracious, everybody's image of a Virginia aristocrat, brought it back its respectability.

Racing was exciting again. Racing was proper.

But horses come and go. Some of them race no more than a year or two. What of the men and women who work on these transients throughout the days, the weeks, the months, the years, in that enclave beyond the shrubs of the racecourse known variously as the barn area, the backside, and the backstretch? Not much is known about them.

And what about the jockeys who ride these horses day-in, day-out? Not much is known about them, either, except that they are short. As people, as individuals, they seem not to count. There is widespread heartbreak when a Joe Namath twists his knee, but when a jockey is thrown from his mount and is carried off with a broken back, the concern is usually for the horse, and then largely because he did not finish to pay for the bet placed on him. The best most jockeys can hope for in such cases is the concern of a few spectators who say something like this: "Who got thrown . . . Was it the Three?"

Yet jockeys are sharply disciplined workmen and perhaps the most heroic of athletes, their lives always in danger. Some of them climb up on their horses with disabilities that are just short of crippling. One rider, for example, underwent open heart surgery at the age of six months, broke his back in his first year of riding, and is still riding.

Certainly every sport has its risks. The football player can expect concussions and torn knee cartilages, the hockey player must be careful of flying pucks and sticks, the baseball player must contend with being beaned and spiked — but none of them has ever been kicked in the head by a thousand pound animal traveling at some forty miles an hour, or lived with the threat of it happening.

Every sport has its names, names that embody the sport. Ruth — baseball. Richard — hockey. Unitas — football. Palmer — golf. These names symbolize a sport, define an era. In racing the names are distant and enigmatic. Bill Shoemaker. Johnny Longden. Eddie Arcaro. Steve Brooks. Bill Hartack. They have a hard, solid ring to them, these names, and though some of us may have a hard time placing them and distinguishing them, we nonetheless greet their mention with a tinge of romance and would peruse a listing of them with the same sense of nostalgia as when reading off a schedule of ancient trains.

If nothing else, they are American. Uniquely so. They hark back to the days of Damon Runyon, when he humorously but faithfully exposed racing's language, its codes, its manners, portrayed its people, invariably losers, and gave it a shading that elevated it to folklore. These five men, two of them — Shoemaker and Hartack — still riding, were major figures when Hemingway made literature of sports writing and Red Smith was making his reputation as racing's most eloquent spokesman.

Modern thoroughbred racing, an English sport, was imported to America in its present form no more than some ninety years ago, and not until Shoemaker, Longden, Arcaro, Brooks, Hartack, and a few others arrived did it have its own character. With Arcaro's brilliance in pacing, Shoemaker's finesse (with his light touch and sensitive hands, Shoemaker plays his horses like Serkin plays a Beethoven piano concerto), and Brooks' daredevil escapes from the gate, American thoroughbred racing had its own interpretation, its own expression.

Each of these five men would go on to win 4,000 races or more and become a charter member in racing's most exclusive club — the club of 4,000.

While Secretariat was flashing through racing's firmament, an event perhaps more important to racing than the Triple Crown was taking shape at Monmouth Park in New Jersey. Walter Blum was closing in on 4,000 wins, and though still in peak form, Walter Blum was a vestige of the Brooks-Arcaro epoch. On Wednesday, July 25, Walter Blum stood at a figure five short of 4,000. To appreciate fully the meaning of this achievement it should be emphasized that while nine horses have won the Triple Crown, only five riders have won 4,000 races or more — before Walter Blum made it six.

The Monmouth Park backstretch resembles the backstretch of any major thoroughbred racetrack, spreading about three-quarters of a mile along the width and two miles along the length, except that in Monmouth's case a railroad track cuts off about a third of the backstretch into a region of unusual serenity. Within the entire backstretch, barracks-style shed rows stand outspread along the width and length. Each shed row consists of anywhere from one to forty horses.

Of the thousand-plus horses on the grounds, some are of stakes caliber but most are claimers. Claimers, of course, are horses that run in races with a price tag, the amount set by their trainer. They can be bought, that is, claimed, moments before a race by any trainer who has run at least one horse of his own during the meeting. Every trainer who enters his horse in a claiming race accepts the risk of losing it. This, naturally, discourages a trainer from entering a top horse against lesser competition, thus assuring most claiming races of being run among horses of equal caliber.

Every shed row is presided over by a trainer, who rules over the grooms, the exercise boys and girls, and the hotwalkers. Though one's job frequently overlaps another's, each groom usually takes care of three horses. His duties include feeding, mucking, bandaging, hosing, administering medicine, and keeping the trainer informed as to each horse's condition. The spotting of an overnight ailment, recognizing when the horse is not doing (eating) his usual amount, is perhaps the groom's paramount responsibility. The exercise boys and girls are one of three things: active jockeys, aspiring jockeys, failed jockeys. Some of them work horses in the mornings and pony in the afternoons, and a few of them work the afternoons as jockey valets. The hotwalkers are at the bottom of the rung. They are men and women who are coming up in their careers, or going down. In walking one horse after another around the shed row for a half hour after each has been worked and hosed, a hotwalker has plenty of time to think about the course his life is taking.

The backstretch, with some of its men in high boots and ten-gallon hats, its roads of dirt, its long patches of grazing greens, its blacksmiths and veterinarians scurrying from barn to barn, its small village in the center, is an anachronism resembling a frontier town of the old wild west. There are men and women here who have never ventured into the "outside." Here physical strength and craftiness are still honored, and a man can spit and curse without fear of recrimination, play a hand of cards in a room filled with smoke, noise, and sweat, and choose his friends from among people who understand huntin' and fishin'. These are rugged people. They smile for the man in the suit but save their respect for the youngster who dares to enter the stall of a rank, back-kicking horse or for the jockey who is back exercising horses the morning after a bad spill.

In this society where "Past Performance" is the measure of a man as well as of a horse, Walter Blum is certainly an honored member. Beneath a front of nonchalance and affability, there is about him a quiet toughness that has granted him some twenty years of success in a line of work that destroys most men after five. There are definitely two sides to the man. Backside he can wisecrack with the best of them. The public, and private, Walter Blum is a man of polish and class. He counts among his friends famous men and women of politics and entertainment. He lives with his wife and two sons in a grand home in one of the more exclusive sections of Cherry Hill, New Jersey, an exclusive township to begin with. He is a sharp dresser, he drives a fancy car, and he is recognized, sought after, and pointed at in every section of the country he works.

Walter Blum is one of the few jockeys who can be said to be famous. In his twenty-some years of riding he has thrilled millions with his pumping, front-running style, aboard horses the likes of Kelso, Gun Bow, Affectionately, Icecapade, Shecky Greene, and Mr. Prospector, to name a handful among thousands. The name "Walter Blum" on an afternoon's program pops out and electrifies and is an assurance of quality and excitement. "Blum's ridin' today!"

As a horseman, allowing for differences in style, he is on a par with Arcaro and Brooks, and, indeed, he is the rider who bridges the gap between that generation and the generation of the Latins, represented largely by Braulio Baeza, Laffit Pincay, Jr., Jorge Velasquez, and Jacinto Vasquez — front-runners in the group that is almost systematically taking over American thoroughbred racing.

In the week of Walter Blum's 4,000 the men and women of the Monmouth Park backstretch went about their work routinely, the men and women in the stands played their horses as usual, but an awareness that something extraordinary — perhaps the closing of an era — was taking place, was inescapable.

Chapter 2

The Mexican rider Humberto Gracia had just come from the shed row of Jose deMurguiondo, for whom he'd been exercising horses. It was still quite early, and there would be more horses to exercise. Humberto Gracia sipped iced tea in the track kitchen. He was sweaty and kept tugging at his jersey. A green line of perspiration and dye from the riding helmet was visible on his forehead.

"I wish Blum the best," he said. "But 4,000, it means nothing to me."

He had no time to worry about Walter Blum. He had Humberto Gracia to worry about.

Yes, he said, to be approaching 4,000 meant that one was a good rider, and Blum was a good rider, but there were at least a dozen other riders he could mention who were just as good as Blum — himself included, if given half the chance.

"My problem," he said, "is that I am not too well known. So the trainers and the owners expect much more from someone like me, more than they would expect from Walter Blum or Michael Hole. If after a race Walter Blum explains to the trainer that the horse had been chicken, the trainer believes him, and that is all. That is all there is. No more is said. A rider like me, he has to take chances. To tell a trainer that the horse was afraid to go into the hole is not enough. They expect you to take chances. So I take the chances. I must, to make a name for myself."

Humberto Gracia was just getting around to making a name for himself. A bad time with immigration had held him back, impeded his progress. For years he'd had no success in obtaining a permanent visa to the United States. Three months at a time was all he could get — then it was time to go back to Mexico and apply all over again.

Often the time to go back was just when he was beginning to make good. When here, he rode Kentucky, he rode Chicago, he rode Philadelphia, he rode Jersey. He'd pick the track that was having dates and ask for permission to ride.

That in itself posed no problem; having won over 700 races in Mexico, he had the credentials. Once he was the leading rider in Mexico, and the years he wasn't first, he was second or third. Usually behind Carlos Barrera.

And when he'd start doing well, it was time to go back. If he forgot the expiration date of his visa by a day or two, men in dark suits with thin briefcases would come backside to remind him. Now he had the permanent visa, but it was like starting from scratch. It was as though he were an apprentice.

"Jose deMurguiondo has been very good to me," Gracia said. "He has been giving me the opportunities."

During this Monmouth meeting Maryland trainer Jose deMurguiondo was serving as Humberto Gracia's unofficial patron. Gracia was not under contract to deMurguiondo. He simply got first call, and he was expected, in return, to work deMurguiondo's horses in the morning. Jose deMurguiondo ran what he liked to call a family operation, employing the full-time services of his wife and children, not to mention various dogs and cats. Mornings he could often be seen reclining on an easy chair outside the tack room of his shed row, and neighboring trainers, among them Harvey Rosenblatt, unaware that he was nursing a heart condition that developed from taking the horses too seriously, marveled over his even temperament.

Jose deMurguiondo had a specific reason for using the Latins. "The American riders are all right," he says. "But after a while they get to being too complacent. They start off a meet real good, get a few wins, and then in the mornings you don't see them around anymore.

"Me, I'm a competitive sort. I like my riders hungry. There's nothing beats a hungry rider. He'll run close along the rail. He'll break through that hole. If there's no room between horses, by heaven he'll make room. He'll take the chances nobody else will. That's why every year I'll start off a new rider from, say, Panama or Mexico. They come here, and they're hungry. I started off quite a few boys that way, Latin boys, and they went on to win big stakes. I drop them soon as they start to getting bigheaded. They start to doing real good, some of them, and before you know it you don't see them around mornings, either. Anyway, this year I'm using Gracia because he's not afraid of work and he's willing and he's not afraid to take chances. If he keeps going the way he is, he's going to be a good one."

Manuel Cedeno sat down next to Gracia. After the two exchanged smiles and a few words in Spanish, Gracia introduced his countryman. Cedeno nodded, shyly. He spoke no English. He drank his coffee in silence.

Gracia said, "To make good in this country, to get the good mounts in the afternoon, you must work very many horses in the morning. I work ten, maybe eleven. I work some for deMurguiondo, but I work many for others, too. This morning I already worked seven or eight. The established riders work maybe two, three. Maybe four. Sometimes only one.

"So when you work ten, eleven horses in the morning, this makes you very tired for the afternoon. But you must. The pressure. The pressure is very tough in this country. There are so many riders from all over, and one is as good as the next. But the money is very good. Very, very good. I left Mexico because there was no money. In Mexico it is very tough for the rider because the only way to make money is to win. The guarantee for each mount is about seventeen dollars and about one hundred and fifty for a winner. So with a spread like this everybody is trying very hard to win and the riding is much rougher, much tighter."

Humberto Gracia learned his riding from Mexico's champion polo player Memo Gracida (likewise Carlos Barrera's tutor). Even after he had grasped the fundamentals and, later, the subtleties of artful horsemanship, Gracia was still not sure that riding horses was a wise choice for a career. So he finished high school and took a year of courses at the University of Mexico toward a law career. But, according to Gracia, he was too short to be a lawyer. So he became a rider and a steady fixture in Mexico's only thoroughbred racetrack, Hipodromo-de-las-Americas.

The kitchen (called the kitchen but actually a cafeteria the size of two basketball courts) was now filled from end to end, and the noise was a continuous drone. This, the eight to eight-thirty break, was a time when the serious business of separating fact from gossip was undertaken, when jokes were told and information sought — which horses were well intended for the afternoon and which were just being given a race, for example. Sometimes when a trainer would not give you a straight answer, you sidled up to a vet to see if he had something hot, or you checked out the blacksmith, or the guy who pulled the horse's teeth. You got to know your sources.

Ten o'clock until about noon was another hectic period in the kitchen, though some trainers preferred to while away the hours before post in the Horseman's Lounge, playing poker and knock-rummy for stakes much too high for grooms and hotwalkers. (A sign in the kitchen, as you approached the cash register, read "Eat Your Betting Money, But Never Bet Your Eating Money.")

Pete Mikos was carrying a tray of breakfast. Pete Mikos was an assistant to one of the leading trainers in the country, Danny Perlsweig.

"Getting the good mounts?" he asked Gracia as he joined the table.

"Oh, yes," he said. "I ride a good horse in the first race this afternoon. Amberco."

"Jolin's horse?"

"Yes."

"You think you got a shot?"

"Very definitely."

"What about you, Manuel?" Pete said.

Manuel Cedeno smiled and shrugged.

"Manuel," Pete said, "you're a damn good rider. You're real good."

"Thank you very much."

"Your only trouble is you can't speak English. That's why you're not getting the mounts."

Manuel Cedeno smiled and shrugged.

"You gotta learn English, Manuel," Pete said.

Turning to Humberto Gracia, he said, "I ran into Ronnie outside. He's looking for you."

Ronnie was Humberto's brother; more important, Ronnie was Humberto's agent. And Ronnie was all right as an agent, getting his brother more and more mounts each day. Of the two, it was Humberto who had the charm. Humberto, as a matter of fact, would have made a fine agent. He had a very accommodating nature, he was quick with a smile, and he had the bearing and style of a Spanish aristocrat. When he wore his riding helmet, all you saw were passionate black eyes and keyboard-white teeth. Brother Ronnie was the worrier — perhaps to be expected of an agent, especially one so young and inexperienced. He'd been at the job, which demanded glibness and wit, not even a year, and it takes more than a year to get the hang of the politics involved in getting mounts. Usually he could be found roaming the backstretch in the morning — the clubhouse in the afternoon — with a glum, worried expression.

Humberto Gracia excused himself. He said he was going out to find his brother. Manuel Cedeno followed behind.

Pete Mikos then joined another table, where some of his friends were seated. One of his friends was Freddie, a former trainer who had had a shed row of some forty two-year-olds. A heart attack had put him out of business. For one reason or another he was ineligible for the various monetary benefits that come to a man recuperating from a serious illness. So now he was a groom, or at least he was trying to be. He could be found in the track kitchen every morning, sitting over a cold cup of coffee, looking for the trainer who would take a chance on a sick old man.

What was up with Cedeno? Freddie wanted to know.

Pete said that Cedeno was still not getting the mounts a rider of his abilities deserved. "If the mother learned some English, he'd be okay. Like Danny used him once and he run a good race, but after the race when Danny asked him what had happened — Was he boxed in? Did he still have a lot of horse under him in the stretch? Did the horse have a problem? — Cedeno couldn't answer. So Danny never rode him again."

"You can't ask the horse," Freddie said.

Some of the grooms around the table were engrossed in the *Daily Racing Form.*

"Did Gracia tell you anything?" a groom named Stanley asked Pete Mikos.

"He said he thought he had a shot in the first."

"Amberco," Stanley said, his paper spread out over his food. "Maybe. What about your horse? He got a shot in the third?"

"Hows The King, baby," Pete said. "Are you kidding? Wire to wire. Blum's on him."

"Yeah, Blum. He's got a couple of good ones today. Shit, he only needs five to get his 4,000."

"Maybe he'll get 'em today. If anybody can do it, he can."

"Naw, he ain't gonna win no five today. If I know Blum, he's gonna wait till Saturday, when the stands are full."

"Come on. Blum don't ride that way. He's an honest jock."

The discussion then touched on jockeys of another sort, like the one who had recently been ruled off in Florida after he had been caught with a battery. The joint was found in his riding knot. The only surprise was that he had not been caught sooner. At Liberty Bell Racetrack in Philadelphia, during the recent meeting there, he had mentioned his using a joint so frequently and boastfully that the information was just short of public knowledge. Anyway, when he arrived in Florida, they had been waiting for him. At the first suspicion they had had him dismount at the starting gate, searched him, and found nothing on him. Then — according to the story — when he had gotten up on his horse again, he had winked at one of the assistant starters, whose curiosity had been aroused enough to call for another search. This time the officials had gone straight for the riding knot in the reins, a common hiding place for a joint.

"You can always tell when a jock is using a joint," one groom said. "That tail goes swish, swish. When you see that old tail suddenly going up in the air, straight up, you know the jock's using a joint."

Another groom mentioned you also had to watch out for the jock who kept coming wide around the turn for home.

"Sure as shootin' he's got a bet on the horse coming down along the inside."

Pete Mikos, an extremely likable backsider, a young man of high enthusiasm who truly loved his work, was the first to finish breakfast. On his way back to Danny Perlsweig's shed row, where the morning's work was still to be done, he steered a visitor in the direction of Jim O'Brey's shed row.

"Might learn something there," he said.

Chapter 3

James O'Brey, Sr., was in no mood to talk about the race track. "I'm busy," he said. "Some other time."

Would it be all right to follow him around? Was it true that the life of a trainer was nothing but aggravation? Okay. He had nothing against being followed around. But he could not talk about the aggravation of being a trainer. At the moment he was having too much aggravation.

His boy was missing.

"Son of a bitch," Jim O'Brey said. "I never should have paid that boy. Soon as you give them a few dollars they're gone."

He walked over to Marty Greenspan, who was standing by his car, which was still warm.

"How do you like that?" Jim O'Brey said. "Can't find a fucking boy to work the horse."

Jim O'Brey walked back and forth in front of the stationary Marty Greenspan.

Marty Greenspan owned the horse Jim O'Brey couldn't find a boy for: MistyPano. Marty Greenspan, a liquor distributor in South Jersey, owned two horses that were trained by Jim O'Brey,

MistyPano and Mitey Jet. You knew Marty Greenspan was an owner of horses by the way he dressed. He wore a suit.

A teenage girl walking a horse for Jim O'Brey stopped in midstride and said, "Mr. O'Brey, can I talk to you?"

"What? What?"

"I'm leaving."

"You're leaving? Go."

"No, I don't mean now. I mean after I finish the morning."

"Terrific."

"I'm going to work for the man in the next barn."

"Finish walking this horse, then go work for the man in the next barn."

"He's paying me more money."

"He is, huh? Good for him."

"Mr. O'Brey?"

"What?"

"Can I have my money now?"

"Later. I gotta find a boy to work my horse. Come on, Marty, let's go to the kitchen and scrape up an exercise boy."

"You never should have paid that boy."

A girl wearing a tight sweater drove by slowly in a '71 Camaro.

"Hey, sweetheart, come here a minute," Jim O'Brey said. "Come here, I want to talk to you."

He leaned inside the open window of the car, talking. After the girl had shaken her head a few times, Jim O'Brey rejoined Marty Greenspan in the walk to the kitchen compound.

"You can't see it from here," O'Brey said. "But that broad's built."

"If you hadn't paid that boy we'd be on the track with my horse right now," Marty Greenspan said.

Approaching the kitchen compound, Jim O'Brey said, "I've been written up more than any other trainer in the country. I can show you the clippings. That's right. I'm a colorful character. I do things different. Sure I'm loud. But that's part of being colorful. People know me. When you're colorful people know you and they respect you. They listen to you. A few years ago I was voted trainer of the year. The night they had the dinner for me at

Zaberer's it rained like hell. Cats and dogs were coming from the heavens. Well, more people showed up for that dinner than any year before. I can show you the clippings."

In the kitchen compound Jim O'Brey shouted, "Hey, anybody here can ride a horse? Anybody?"

"Try the kitchen," said Marty Greenspan.

Jim O'Brey tried the kitchen and emerged with Rocco Martin, an apprentice.

"We don't have much time," Jim O'Brey said.

Rocco Martin was going to ride MistyPano in a few days. But if Greenspan and O'Brey had had their choice, they would have gone to Vincent Bracciale, Jr. Bracciale had ridden the mare twice before, in her two most recent races, and had won on her both times. But for the next race he had "prior commitments." Now they were going with Rocco Martin, for the apprentice allowance. (To compensate for his inexperience the apprentice rider is given a weight advantage, and though the specifics vary from state to state, the allowance usually ranges from ten pounds — signified by three asterisks, or bugs, beside his name — to seven pounds, two bugs, to five pounds, one bug, to matriculation, each step taken after the rider has recorded x number of wins.)

Jim O'Brey and Greenspan watched the mare canter onto the main track. They were standing in the backstretch stands.

"Now you watch when he first starts out with her," said O'Brey. "She'll look like she's ready to fall off her feet." The first time around the track the mare indeed looked as if she was going to fall off her feet. She showed no inclination to run, and each stride seemed an effort. Her action was more sideways than forward. "Now watch as she collects herself." For the second go-round the mare was definitely on the muscle, and since this was not supposed to be a blowout, the rider had his hands full holding her back, tugging at the reins, tugging, tugging, yanking the bit with all his strength. Coming around the final turn, she began to pass horses, thinking she was in a race.

Jim O'Brey beamed. "See, I told you."

Rocco Martin said, "I had a lot of horse under me. She started off bad but around the half-mile pole she started to smooth out."

Walking back to the shed row, Jim O'Brey said, "You want to know about racing? I'll tell you about racing."

He hitched up his pants.

"It's not the way it used to be."

Surely, there must be more.

"Well," he said, having trouble keeping his pants up, "when I first started out — I started out years and years and years ago, I used to be a singer, an entertainer — when I first started out, the mob was everywhere. You couldn't do a thing without the mob getting into the act. They used to be very influential. Now not so much anymore, if at all. Now the security is very tight. They got everybody fingerprinted, and if you want to be a trainer or an owner, they check you back to the day you were born. They got a file a mile long on everybody. You can't get away with much these days. Used to be a guy could buy a horse in somebody else's name. It's still done, but they catch you."

Jim O'Brey was back in his shed row in time to learn the news that one of his horses was suffering from paralysis of the vocal chords. The vet said it was not up to him to decide what to do. He would suggest shipping the horse to New Bolton for surgery. The operation might work, and it might not. The chances of the horse's recovering and being able to race again were fifty/fifty. The vet got in his car, started it up, and said to let him know.

Jim O'Brey paced in front of his shed row.

"There you have it," he said. "There's being a trainer for you. Horse isn't even worth the five thousand dollars, never won a race for me, and now he's gonna need surgery. Gonna be out at least two months. When he comes back, who knows if he'll be able to run?

"Who knows if he's even coming back. He may have to be destroyed. Fifty/fifty shit. If I try to sell him, who's gonna wanna buy him? Would I wanna buy a horse with paralyzed vocal chords? So I guess I'll have to ship him to the hospital. He's no good to me this way. Fuck."

Jim O'Brey kicked some dirt.

"You can't do miracles with a horse. Every trainer thinks he can do magic. Miracles. There's no such thing. Every trainer thinks he's different. What a bunch of shit! Listen, every trainer is the same. There's only so much you can do with horses. There are no geniuses. A trainer has got the horses or he don't."

"Mr. O'Brey?" said the hotwalker who was quitting.

"Yeah, what do you want?"

"Can I have my money now?"

"In a minute."

The girl, and the horse she was walking, made another complete circle of the shed row as Jim O'Brey checked his wallet.

"It's going to be time to leave soon," she said, stopping again.

"I'll pay you later," he said.

The girl resumed her hotwalking.

"Come on," said Marty Greenspan. "Let's go have some breakfast."

"Yeah," said Jim O'Brey. "Let's have some eggs."

Chapter 4

Vincent Bracciale, Jr., was sitting alone in the track kitchen, munching on some toast.

"This here guy," said Jim O'Brey, helping himself to the chair next to Bracciale's, "is *the* leading rider, and I don't mean just Monmouth. I mean he's the leading rider in all of North America."

Vincent Bracciale, Jr., did not seem very impressed.

"Ain't that right you fucking bastard?" Jim O'Brey said.

"I don't know about that," Bracciale said. "I think Sandy Hawley may be ahead of me today. I didn't check the papers."

"Well, in my book you're leading rider."

"In wins, yeah. But in money earned, ain't nobody going to catch Pincay."

Even so, Vincent Bracciale, Jr., stood to make well over one hundred and fifty thousand dollars this year (minus approximately 25 percent agent's fee and 10 percent valet fee). He was ninteen years old. Speaking only of those who earn their money through labor, he was probably the wealthiest ninteen year old in — never mind North America — the world. Not bad for a kid who went almost three months without a win after he lost his bug.

He still did not look like much of a winner. (Of course that could be said of any rider early in the morning, out of his silks, in his work clothes.) Sitting in the track kitchen munching on some toast, gulping down his milk, he could easily have been mistaken for a hotwalker or an exercise boy. He didn't even have the presence of a groom. Oval face, unkempt hair, big, round, ingenuous eyes, he looked all of nineteen years — and not a day older.

"It's important for me to be leading rider," he said. "But I don't feel no pressure. I just go out and do what I have to do. Hawley, he comes on strong at the end. I had a good start. I've been lucky. I've been getting the good mounts."

For all his success, he had still to earn the unequivocal respect of backstretch horsemen. Many said lucky was all he was — lucky to have Steve Vaonakis for an agent, extremely fortunate to have John Tammaro for a supporting trainer.

"Tammaro," he said, "got me off real good."

John Tammaro, one of the leading trainers in all of North America, was a former jockey who gained over a hundred pounds after he stopped being a jockey. (Many former jockeys went that way, making up in a year the accumulated weight they couldn't put on in forty.) On a horse trained by Tammaro, ridden by Bracciale, you could hardly lose. But you had to keep in mind Steve Vaonakis. The bug-less Bracciale had gone some seventy races without a win, and though he had been a hot apprentice, it figured that, like most hot apprentices, he was nothing without his bug. Probably 80 percent of all excellent bug boys become excellent hotwalkers and exercise boys after they lose their bug. The typical agent would have given up on Bracciale. But Vaonakis stuck with him, made the rounds with him, talked him up — either because he had that true faith in his boy that most agents profess to have in their boys but don't, or because, a sharp horseman, he gambled on the constancy of the sire, a fine jockey of years past.

Marty Greenspan, who'd been held up in the breakfast procession, yelled, "There's my boy," and joined the table.

Bracciale ignored him.

A groom came over and whispered something in Bracciale's ear He smiled and kept on eating, his eyes never leaving his food, his mind never off the task at hand. The groom straightened up, waiting for a larger response, and when he got none, left.

Marty Greenspan, by nature a very friendly and outgoing man, went into a long story about some horses he'd once owned, pausing every now and then for dramatic effect, and drawing absolutely no enthusiasm from Bracciale.

"Yeah," Bracciale said.

Those who did not say Bracciale's only talent was luck said he had become insufferably bigheaded. (Pete Mikos observed: "What do you expect from kids just off the farm suddenly making a thousand dollars a day?") Bigheaded, perhaps. A generous person, however, would be disposed to define his obduracy as shyness, though he was impatient with strangers. He had no use for persons who could not advance him and as yet had not acquired the nonchalant grace that more experienced athletes display in dealing with members of the press. That would come later, if it came at all. (It never came to Michael Hole.)

On the backstretch you grow up fast and you become a man when others of your generation are still boys. That works to your advantage: you develop early the tough skin that is necessary for survival. On the other hand, the period in life that teaches you manners passes you by.

Luck or whatever, the one thing they could not take away from Bracciale was his success. In a world where you win or you lose, success is everything, and those who possess it are loved, hated, envied, and even feared. (The stewards will think twice before setting down a leading jockey, whereas a washout, for the same infraction, can count on getting "days" as a matter of course.)

Bracciale knew success before he knew failure, which could explain the reluctance of backstretch horsemen to endorse him. Those two, three bad months of his did not figure to men who knew years of failure, and to whom failure always came before success, if success came at all.

Anyway, part envy, part reservation kept Bracciale from being as accepted by men who knew their horses in the morning as he was by men who knew their horses only in the afternoon.

But Number One he was.

To aspiring jockeys he was a magnet. They tried to joke with him. They tried to draw him out, hoping to extract that morsel of wisdom that could change something in them. They patted him on the back, as though success were contagious. So long as he offered any kind of response, they stayed on. Perhaps inadvertently he would drop a hint. Perhaps a word would unlock the secret.

If it was talent, that acquired or inborn knack of doing something on a horse that made a clear difference, of the kind to be found in the Walter Blums and Howard Grants, they would learn. They would watch and they would learn; as they learned from watching Rudy Turcotte that you do not necessarily have to sit high on a horse, that by sitting low, almost touching the saddle, you could perhaps master him even more fully. But if Bracciale's chief quality was luck, if the whole secret was good fortune, there would be nothing to learn.

"I like being Number One," Bracciale said. "It looks good."

Chapter 5

Danny Perlsweig liked to think of himself as a fighting general.

"Some trainers come all dressed up in suits," he said. "They walk around giving orders and never get their hands dirty. They're generals. Me, I'm a fighting general, and I'll probably do it till the day I die."

As any good general would, he paced up and down his shed row surveying his charges. The groom Wanda Gold, an attractive blonde, was applying standing bandages to Mr. Correlation. "This is the star of the stable," Danny Perlsweig said. "He's the best horse we have in the barn. He won the Trenton Handicap at Garden State and the Keystone Handicap at Liberty Bell."

Mr. Correlation, by Correlation out of Sundownette, was a four-year-old liver-chestnut colt. He was owned by Mrs. Robert S. Lytle of Florida. The distance of a mile and seventy yards suited him best. He had great heart and was easily the most popular horse on the grounds. He was a crowd pleaser. He liked to go right to the front and to stay there, and when he was at his best — which was often — he could be headed and come back, drawing away as though it had all been a tease.

Many horsemen believe that on appearance alone there is no telling the common horse from the exceptional. True as this may generally be, Mr. Correlation had easily recognizable nobility. A handsome horse, with intelligent eyes, he stood on long, graceful legs that moved in grand, smooth strides, even on a hotwalking stroll around the shed row.

He was a particular favorite at Garden State, and some horsemen still expressed the suspicion that on at least one occasion the surface there had been sprinkled extra moist for his benefit. He won the Keystone at Liberty Bell in 1:42 flat, setting a thunderous pace of 1:09 and change for the three quarters. He was a thing of beauty to watch, and studying his chart in the *Daily Racing Form* was equally satisfying — those clean "ones" showing all the way across, practically from bottom to top. Frank Lovato, who rode him once (Buck Thornburg was his regular rider), described the feeling of supremacy a jockey had in riding a horse like Mr. Correlation: "When they start coming up to you from behind you just give the knot a little twist, and it's like changing gears." In one of his few six furlong races, at Liberty Bell, he outdistanced his rivals at the wire by seven lengths, doing a time of 1:12 on a sloppy track. Typical was his manner of running — drawing away by three, then by five, then by eight, then catching a breather to hold on by seven. Mr. Correlation made fans of backstretch horsemen by virtue of the fact that he loved to run — a feature rare among most thoroughbreds. Still only a four-year-old, Mr. Correlation had a promising career ahead of him. Yet there had been a time when his career had not seemed so promising. As a weanling in Ocala, Florida, he had been struck by lightning.

Wanda Gold patted him on the face. Mr. Correlation bared his teeth.

"Ah, don't be so mean," Wanda said in a mock pout.

"He's still mad because of the other day," said Pete Mikos.

The other day Mr. Correlation had been in such a hurry to leave the starting gate that he fell to his knees before reaching first stride. Buck Thornburg, nearly thrown, managed to hang on to finish the race — out of the money. Now, in the firehouse next door, there hung a picture of Buck Thornburg almost being thrown and Mr. Correlation on his knees. The picture hung there as an example of a horse with too much heart.

Shorty, Danny Perlsweig's ace groom, who was applying a poultice to one of his horses, ambled by and said to a reporter, "You guys never get it right. You guys always get it wrong."

Danny Perlsweig, who was sorting out his tack room, suggested that the comment be ignored.

"Every shed row has a Shorty," Pete Mikos laughed.

Shorty, in fact, according to the likes of Shorty, knew more about horses than any man dead or alive. Were it not for his forthright manner and lack of interest in matters of attire, he would have made a fine trainer. In other words, he would not do as a trainer because all he cared about was horses. As Pete Mikos would say, an owner liked to have the kind of trainer who he could point to and say: "There's my trainer."

Knowing so much about horses understandably got Shorty into big trouble, especially with Danny Perlsweig. And because he always knew better than Danny Perlsweig, Shorty quit every other day. On the days he did not quit, Danny Perlsweig fired him.

Someday, perhaps, Shorty would find work with a trainer who had some knowledge of horses — but, of course, such a trainer was still to be born. Any groom will tell you that. Aloysius, for example, another Perlsweig groom, felt that most trainers had no consideration for their horses. He felt that very strongly.

"The other day," he said, "I saw a man beating a horse. He was punching away like crazy, hitting the horse on the belly, all over. So I walked up to him, see, I walked up to him, I wasn't afraid, and I said, 'You call yourself a *horseman*?' "

No matter the circumstance, there was never sufficient cause to beat a horse, according to Aloysius. If the horse was unresponsive, it was your fault, your failing as a horseman — and other than as a pejorative, "horseman" was not a term Aloysius threw around lightly.

Aloysius and Shorty shared the same room, next to the tack room. They lived there night and day, and night and day they talked horses. It was said if you were to spend a night and a day with Shorty and Aloysius, you would come away knowing enough about horses to fill an encyclopedia. From Aloysius, who once studied for the priesthood, you would get the chimerical view, and you would learn how the placement of the sun, the moon, and the stars played a role in the outcome of a horse race, and that a horse bearing the number four had been a bad bet ever since the Four Horsemen of the Apocalypse. From Shorty you would get the unswerving practical side, and learn that a surface that was slightly moist — anything but hard, dry, and cuppy — could do more for a horse than the sun, the moon, or the stars, and that if a horse was fit and well intended, it did not matter at all if he was number four or number six — he would be on the board.

Moreover, you would learn from Shorty that rhythm on a horse — in the riding, in the whipping — was what separated the good jockey from the bad jockey, and that when it came to rhythm, there was none the equal of Michael Hole.

(Pete Mikos did not share Shorty's enthusiasm for Michael Hole. He remembered asking Hole, after he had put in a losing performance on a Perlsweig mount, the standard, "What happened?" The reply was equally to the point: "What was supposed to happen?")

Another Perlsweig groom was Louis Goldberg, a physical education graduate of Kent State. He had no plans to become a physical education teacher. He loved the track. He loved the backstretch. His only outside activity was reading war books. War fascinated him. ("I would have become a soldier if it weren't so dangerous.") Someday, if all went well, he would have a shed row of his own. Meanwhile, he was learning.

Pete Mikos was teaching him his first lesson in how to condition a horse new to the barn. "When a new horse comes to the shed row," Pete said, "you never start off feeding him a mixture. You start off feeding him one thing at a time, one day at a time — 'cause if you feed him a mixture and he develops a bad reaction, you'll never know which element was responsible. So each day you add something new, and that way you know what you're doing."

This morning Pete Mikos — who physically resembles

the hockey player Derek Sanderson to a fault — was something of a celebrity along the backstretch. The night before he had performed an act of some daring, having, by means of artificial respiration, breathed life back into a horse, Gator Queen, dying of colic, going at it mouth to mouth all the way to recovery.

"I didn't get to know horses from behind-the-scenes until recently," Pete Mikos said, as he walked along, checking each horse in the stable, including Hows The King, who was "certain to win for Blum this afternoon." "But I sure knew all I wanted to know about horses from the stands.

"My dad and me," he said with amusement, "we weren't like normal people. You know, when you were a kid in New York your father would take you to Yankee Stadium or Ebbets Field. Well, not my father. He took me to Belmont and Aqueduct. I was just a kid, seven, eight, and I used to go crazy, 'cause we'd get to the track soon as it opened, around ten. So there was always about three hours to kill before the races started, and for a kid, you know, three hours of nothing to do but sit is murder.

"My father would say, 'Why are you so restless? Why can't you sit in one place?' He couldn't figure me out. Of course not. He had the *Telegraph* to read and keep him company. What did I have to do?

"So I was all over the place, squirming in my seat, under my seat, everything. I couldn't understand how a guy could sit and read the same paper, the same page, all morning.

"But when the races started I was more excited than any kid could be. In my house the heroes weren't Mickey Mantle or Duke Snider. They were Arcaro, Shoemaker, Longden. My dad and me, hell, we'd sit up there, way up there, in the grandstand, and we'd look down at the jockeys getting off their mounts — we didn't know anything about trainers or grooms or that there even was such a thing as a backstretch — and we'd wonder who you had to be to meet these guys. They were real heroes."

Pete became his father's hero when he worked his way up to assistant trainer for Danny Perlsweig. The other Mikos son didn't do as well. He became a doctor.

Danny Perlsweig was observing one of his horses being breezed around the oval.

"I think Blum will win for me today on Hows The King," he said. "The horse was second the other day here, and I think he should improve off that effort. Blum, he's a good rider, and he's a gentleman. He's been riding for me like twenty years, ever since he broke his maiden.

"I used to be a jockey myself. I did my riding up and down the East Coast: New Jersey, Maryland. I quit riding 'cause I was starting to ride a lot of bad horses. Just couldn't get any good horses to ride. Now I wasn't the greatest rider."

In 1967 Danny Perlsweig was the leading trainer in New Jersey. He was usually someplace near the top.

"I always wanted to become a horse trainer, but I wasn't successful from the word go. I did okay. But I didn't have the horses. I started with one horse I bought myself, here in Monmouth Park, June First, 1954. I bought a horse of my own, and ironically his name was Dandy Dan. Dandy Dan."

He bought the horse from Doc Colando for $2,500.

"I never won a race with the horse. I ran him eighteen times. He got fifteen checks for me. He was eight seconds, and seven thirds, and he never won a race — and I lost him. The next time the horse run he won. I darn near quit."

Old friends still called Danny Perlsweig Dandy Dan. Horsemen — not particularly a sentimental bunch — never forget that first horse, in much the same way a woman never forgets her first love. Some horsemen are named forever after the horse that broke their maiden. Aloysius, actually Robert Zednick, named himself Aloysius in nostalgic tribute to the horse that broke his maiden as a groom.

"Then," said Danny Perlsweig, "I started picking up a horse here, a horse there, for different people. It was tough breaking in because the stall situation is so tough. Naturally they give the stalls to the people who have been there, and usually the only way you can break in is if you have a couple of horses who can run. Then they give you some stalls, possibly."

Danny Perlsweig shook his head. The boy breezing his horse

was letting him out too much. The horse was being timed by the clockers at the other end. Clockers are not greatly respected along the backstretch. The belief is that they list erroneous times intentionally. If a horse has a terrific workout, doing three furlongs in, say, .34, they list it at, say, .36, so that they can place a bet on it at higher odds.

"Anyway," Danny Perlsweig said, "my career steadily went up. I fortunately have done very well in racing. I'm quite happy with racing, and as a trainer I've been fairly successful. In fact, I think I've been very successful.

"But you never know. Anything can happen — like losing all your horses and going out of business, by having all your horses claimed or by having all your horses break down. You can get wiped out quickly. One of the worst things that can happen to you is a fire. Happened in Hialeah. Del Carroll and Eddie Yowell lost a lot of horses. A few years ago Benny Perkins was completely wiped out at Garden State.

"But you think about the positive. I think every trainer wants to win the Kentucky Derby, possibly the Triple Crown. Regardless of what races you win, I think if you win the Triple Crown this is the height of success. What you need are the horses.

"A good horse makes a good trainer. Sunny Jim Fitzsimmons had a famous expression: A shotgun is dangerous in anybody's hands, and so is a good horse.

"But there is that element of luck. I'm a great believer in luck. Lou Wolfson — I'm an expression man, by the way — Lou Wolfson had an expression years ago, when he was really going big. When somebody asked him what he owed his success to, luck or skill, he said, 'Hundred percent luck, the rest was skill.'

"That goes for jockeys. That goes for trainers. I'm not saying you don't need skill, but luck is very important. And a rider is only as good as his horse. I'd say on a horse a jockey counts no more than 10 percent.

"From experience I can say it's much easier being a rider than being a trainer. A rider, he don't have all the heartaches of help, all the problems of horses going lame. A rider will ride a horse for me, for instance, and my horse will get all cut up in the race. The rider gets off him and takes a shower. I got to live with the son of a bitch.

"But there is a difference in riders, and I'll always use the top riders. I train a public stable. I train for various people. To keep me out of hot water, to keep things going good, I prefer to use the best riders I could possibly use.

"One of my theories on riders is this: if I use a top rider and he gets beat two or three lengths there's usually nothing said — talking about the owner. If I use an inferior rider and he gets beat a nose and the horse runs the best race of his life, the owner probably says, 'Gee, if ya had Arcaro on that horse . . .' "

Or Blum.

Chapter 6

For Walter Blum the pointing and the shouting start as soon as he steps out of his silver-gray Mercedes.

"There's Walter Blum!"

"Hey, Walter! Hey, Walt! Hey, Blum!"

This is the second part of the day for Walter Blum. The first part started around 7:00 A.M., at which time, in the kitchen, he had a breakfast of toast — one slice — and coffee. Except for a reasonably filling meal in the evening, that is his entire daily diet. During breakfast he goes over the *Daily Racing Form*, doing his handicapping. ("Jockeys, on the whole, are the worst handicappers in the world. Right at the top of the list is me.") Not being a bettor, he handicaps for the purpose of evaluating his chances. When he is through reading the charts, he reads the paper for its news. Occasionally he will pick up an *Inquirer* and read what Russ Harris has to say. Or a *Daily News* to read what Steve Klessel has to say. Or, in the evening, an *Evening Bulletin* to read what Bill Fidati has to say. These are among the finest Turf writers in the country, and Blum gets along well with newsmen — the exceptions being those who dabble in "hundred-dollar words."

When he is done with breakfast, he gets on a horse or two. Around ten, he goes home and gets some sleep, then heads back so that he can be in the jockeys' room by around noon.

A woman dressed in fancy pants turns to a man in a plaid jacket and white shoes: "Harry, is that *Walter Blum*?"

"Looks like him."

"Go up to him, Harry. Ask him something."

Walter Blum keeps on walking, eyes fixed to anything pointing straight ahead. Frontside, a jockey can't be too careful, especially one so prominent as Walter Blum. A casual moment with the wrong company, the wrong element, can cost him days. Once, years ago at Santa Anita, at a time when he thought riding horses was all there was to being a jockey, Walter Blum drew a long suspension for having a word or two with persons of criminal repute. Trouble was, nobody told Walter Blum they were persons of criminal repute — at least not until the damage had been done. Walter Blum thought they were three guys who just happened to be very friendly. Yet nothing that he said, nothing that the newspapers wrote — practically all the reporters came to his defense, some rising to great passion and indignation — could lift the suspension. The suspension stuck, and Walter Blum learned himself a lesson.

Undesirables are as much a part of racetrack life as the horses. They come in the form of touts, pickpockets, bookies, and ten-percenters. They make up a small portion of the race-going public, but there are enough of them around to give the sport a bad name.

The man who has been parking Walter Blum's car for years and years said, "You son of a bitch, you can't park here."

This is his way of being friendly.

"I can't, huh? I'll push your face in."

This is Walter Blum's way of being friendly.

"Yeah? I'll knock your fucking teeth out." To somebody else, when Blum was out of hearing range, he said, "Best there is."

The legitimate, licensed, tip sheet hucksters come alive when Walter Blum passes by.

"Walter, baby!"

"Hey, Walter! Want the Double?"

"Hey, Blum! Here's the Double!"

"Hey, Mousey! Know anything?"

Blum smiled. "I don't know nothing. You guys don't know nothing, either."

"Yeah, but we pretend we do."

This drew great laughter, probably because it was the only time you would ever hear such an admission.

A man wearing a scarf — it is about ninety degrees — tried to catch up with Blum. When he did, he was all nerves. He was about to make a prepared statement, and his future obviously depended on it coming out as rehearsed. "Blum," he said. "Know anything?"

Blum shrugged and kept on walking.

Another man, this one helping himself along with a cane, said, "Mousey, in the fourth, who ya got to beat?"

"Got to beat them all."

The man with the cane nodded approvingly. From anyone else this would have been a wisecrack. From Walter Blum it was a revelation.

"Here, Walter," he said, "here's a paper."

Blum took the paper and said thanks. Both the man with the cane and Walter Blum had benefited from the exchange. The man with the cane could now say he had spoken to Walter Blum. He could think to himself, I gave Walter Blum a newspaper, so he is my friend. Maybe next time he will remember me and tell me something. Walter Blum, for his part, saved himself ten cents. This means a great deal to someone making around one hundred and twenty five thousand dollars a year.

Tom Kelly, the clerk of scales, liked to have his men report in at the proper weight. It was a matter of pride with him. The riders who came in at the proper weight were his boys.

Walter Blum, as he had expected, was two pounds over. He was expected to do 113.

For Walter Blum, as well as for many others, the hotbox is the most unpleasant part of being a jockey. "Let me tell you it's miserable," he said. "It's sheer torture. If anybody ever talks to you about the glamour of racing, tell them about the hotbox."

The hotbox emits dry heat, reaching a temperature of about 170°. Strangers to the jockeys' room are often invited to spend a few moments in the hotbox, as a means of initiation. There are tales of newsmen and other types of big shots who passed out in the hotbox rather than admit that the heat was too much. Always good for a laugh.

"If I want to take off two pounds," said Blum, "I might have to stay in the hotbox an hour and a half."

Of course, you can't stay in there all that time. "I'll stay in there for maybe fifteen minutes, come out, get some air, go back in, come out, have a cigarette, go back — at intervals of fifteen minutes. In about an hour and a half you can get about two pounds off. I can.

"But not only is it miserable, it's very taxing. When I come out of a sauna or a steam bath, first thing I want to do is lay down and go to sleep. That's what I would love to do. As it is, I've got to go to work."

On the whole, however, in terms of weight, Walter Blum is rather fortunate.

"Some boys," he said, "have a much tougher time than me. Me, instead of enduring the hotbox I just don't eat. So usually I'm okay. I do my 113. When I was an apprentice I could do 105, 106. As I progressed through the years I got to where I couldn't do 110 anymore. I filled out from riding. I grew up and I got muscular. I gained maybe 10 pounds, and I found doing 110 tough. Finally now I do 113. But some boys have trouble doing 114, 115. They have to go into the hotbox every day. I know four jockeys that I'll bet in their careers have taken off 5,000 pounds apiece in the hotbox: Eric Guerin, Ray Broussard, Pete Anderson, Jimmy Nichols.

"Some jockeys, they get up in the morning knowing that they've got to go hit that box, and me, I think I would rather find something else to do. To me that's disgusting, to have that to look forward to every day. I just wouldn't want to do it."

Nick Pompilio was rubbing down the Hungarian rider Paul Kallai. Nick Pompilio had been a masseur for some thirty years.

Most of those years he spent at the YMHA in Philadelphia, but he had been a masseur on the Jersey circuit long enough to have kneaded and pounded the flesh of some of the most illustrious names in racing.

"More wintergreen," said Paul Kallai. "More wintergreen. Don't be stingy with the wintergreen, modderfock."

Paul Kallai had just come off the tennis court. As a tennis player, he is of professional caliber, and when it comes to Ping-Pong only Walter Blum can be mentioned in the same breath. Paul Kallai is a complete athlete. He is built like a boxer and has, in fact, been boxing off and on since the age of thirteen. Though riding is his full-time vocation, Kallai still finds the time to get in a bout or two against a professional — the most recent of which, at the Spectrum in Philadelphia, he lost by a controversial split decision.

Paul Kallai was perhaps the strongest rider on the circuit, any circuit, and had a temper to match. When he first came here from Hungary — he left in time to miss out on the Revolution and went back for a visit in time to learn that the Russians had taken all the thoroughbreds — he used to make a habit of mixing it up with jockeys who had earned his displeasure. Now he got on well with his peers, but the fans — the fans were another story.

"The fans, they're disgusting," Paul Kallai said. "They throw tickets in your face. Modderfockers. They think tickets don't hurt. Look, look my eyelids. I have my eyelids torn and stitched from tickets, from people throwing losing tickets in my face. What do they think? They think you can carry the horse across the finish line? If the horse don't want to run, you cannot carry him across the finish line. So you walk by the fans, and they throw a whole hand of tickets in your face."

Nick Pompilio said, "Remember that guy, a while back, that slugged you in the face when you were coming down the tunnel?"

"I'm walking to the tunnel," said Kallai, "and this guy, he yells out my name. 'Hey, Kallai,' he yells. I turn around. Modderfock. He smacks me right in the face with a clenched fist. I wasn't ready so he got me straight on. Flush. I was bleeding like crazy."

"He sure was a big guy."

"Modderfocker. I tried to get him back. So what happens.

Two guys come do me a favor. They come around me and hold back my arms. I went back in the jockey room, put on my clothes, and went looking for the modderfocker in the parking lot. He was nowhere. I never seen him again."

A rider who had just come in from New York stepped out of the hotbox to get some air. He took a cube of ice out of the bucket, sucked on it, rolling it around in his mouth like candy, removed the cube of ice, sat down on the tile, bending his body forward, and began to flip.

Like most jockeys to whom flipping is a daily routine, he did not require a finger stuck down his throat. The puke came out on demand. After flipping, he cooled his mouth with ice, walked around a bit, shivering, and went back into the hotbox.

"Jockeys," said Paul Kallai, "entertain more people than anybody, and still nobody considers them entertainers. Jockeys are the best-conditioned athletes, and still nobody considers them athletes."

"I don't know about that," said Nick Pompilio, digging away. "I mean I don't know about jockeys being the best-conditioned athletes."

"Okay, modderfock. You call a baseball player an athlete? Anybody can pick up a bat and hit a ball. But who can ride a horse?"

"Football players are pretty well conditioned."

"Sure, but what football player has to get up five in the morning, work horses who weigh a thousand pounds, keep on a diet that has no food, then flip what they do eat, spend two hours in the sweatbox every day, then go out and ride a whole afternoon?"

Paul Kallai nodded in the direction of the jockeys in the hotbox.

"Me," he said, "I never go in the sweatbox. I lose weight, I lose all the weight I want playing tennis. Keeps you fit. Keeps you healthy. You don't get sick, and you don't walk around dizzy all the time."

When Nick Pompilio was done, Paul Kallai rolled himself up into a ball. As he unfurled himself, he tuned and flexed each muscle. He was obviously a man who knew the worth of his body. "When you go out there," he said, "you want to be as loose as you can."

Scars, from riding accidents, from car accidents, from lawn mower accidents, were evident on every part of his body. "Ever see anybody with so many scars?" he said. He jumped off the table in one clean motion, landing on his feet in the manner of a high-wire artist. "Riding is dangerous all right," he said. "That's why riders play around with women so much. Everything in a rider's life is fast. He goes out there, and he can get killed. You never know how much time you have." After completing a somersault, he said, "I love life. I love to ride. I love to ride horses. I love it."

Wednesday Afternoon

Chapter 7

Jim Raftery was standing on the porch of the administration building, which gave an overall view of the jockeys' room, the adjoining paddock, the walking ring, and the path that led to the tunnel. "There's Cab Calloway," he said. Jim Raftery was the official track photographer and he knew everybody — everybody who needed knowing. "In California," he said, "that's where you see the stars. The stars, they all love racing." Cab Calloway is a big racing fan. So, of course, is Burt Bacharach, who has a fortune in thoroughbreds and uses Willie Shoemaker as his rider.

Jim Raftery also knew every jockey worth knowing, and perhaps his favorite was Walter Blum. "Nobody's got class like Walter Blum," he said. He could tell you a million stories about the guy, about how he regularly gave his time and energy to all manner of worthy causes, and, of course, nobody could forget the hilarious performances he put on for crippled children, dressed up there on the stage like a woman, doing all kinds of funny women things. Jim Raftery had seen it all. He had taken the pictures.

There was one picture he could not wait to take. That would be of Walter Blum in the winner's circle, holding up a sign that read "4,000." The sign was already lettered, and it sat hidden in the publicity office, waiting.

Walter Blum was listed on Norkin in the first race, and the early arrivals, after finding a spot warmed by the sun, leafed the *Daily Racing Form* to the proper page, then studied the charts of the various horses, among them Norkin, an Argentine import that had come in fifth by seven lengths in his last race. The most you could say of that horse was that he could surprise.

Horse racing is the grand attraction that it is because for all its complications it is still, always, a story with a beginning and an end. At the top of the afternoon, before the first race, when his *Racing Form* is still neat, all pages in place, folded impeccably along the length, the program crisp, fresh, and cool, the horses in the paddock jaunty with anticipation, nothing and nobody is more alive and full of life than the horseplayer.

The mistakes of the day before are forgotten, behind. (A day of mistakes it had been, of that you could always be sure. But the true horseplayer never blames a bad day on the horses or on the jockeys. Neither does he fault luck. The fault is his and his alone, and when he is feeling kindly toward himself, he puts it all down as simple miscalculation; when angry, plain stupidity.)

The stupid mistakes are what sting, and playing the favorite with the second choice in an exacta, as he had the day before, was what he had to forget. That, he'd known, was playing it stupid. That was playing it obvious. Right into their hands. That's the way they wanted him to play it — obvious. Well, that's the way the suckers played it. There was always an element of surprise, of course, to make it interesting. Yet there is no such thing as surprise, really. Everything makes sense. Everything follows logic. The horse that wins is the horse that is going to win — ever since this morning, ever since ten thousand years ago. All that remains is to figure it out. Surprises come to those who are unprepared, to those who show no imagination, to those who choose the obvious. In racing, the obvious never happens. Well, yes it does. But only when you are looking for the surprise.

Walter Blum in the first race of a card is always dangerous.

The thinking is that — unless there is something very hot in the first — a jockey saves himself for later, when the purses are bigger and the horses truer to form. In the first race, the second race, and the ninth race, you have your cheapies — as cheap as they can come.

The not-so-well-known truth is that in those races you also have your stuck horses — horses that are sore, lame, entered in a race for the sake of padding the field, on the demand of the Association and the compliance of the trainer. Yet stuck horses are not indigenous to the first, second, and ninth races. Stuck horses can be found in any race. It is for the trainer and the Association to know and for the horseplayer to find out.

Along the backstretch, stuck horses are the shame of all grooms who take their horses seriously, and who have to seal their lips and turn the other way when they know a horse that can hardly walk is being sent out to run. The Young Turks, counting the days when the sport will be theirs, make vows that no horse under their care will ever be sacrificed to the Association.

That remains to be seen. There always will be the matter of getting along with the Association. There always is the chance that the trainer who falls from the good graces of the Association will have a hard time getting stalls the next time around. Sooner or later (exceptions proving the rule), even the most conscientious trainer learns to live with an unassailable fact of racetrack life: expediency.

On Walter Blum, however, you know you are getting your money's worth. He has developed through the years, frontside and backside, the reputation of getting on only those horses that are ready and well intended. So in this, the first race of the afternoon, on Norkin, a horse that should have gone off at much higher odds, he went off at 10 to 1.

Breaking from the nine post, Norkin went wide immediately but had enough early speed to stay within a half length of the leader along the backstretch, four horses back — gradually to fade from contention. The leader, Amberco, Humberto Gracia up, broke smoothly and easily from the inside, opening up a length and a half lead before the quarter. Rounding the far turn, he disposed of Capt. Bennington, then Smart Lad. Leaving the quarter pole for the stretch, he was engaged by Smart Lad, and Humberto Gracia drew his mount in tight along the rail, dangerously close, finally going to the whip on both sides, passing the whip from left hand to right by way of clenched teeth, swiftly, making the transfer of whip from hand to mouth to hand, then back again, hand to mouth to hand, all in one blurry motion, finishing ahead of the field by five lengths.

"Them Panamanians again," somebody grumbled.

Ever since the advent of Ycaza and Baeza, every Latin American rider was a Panamanian, no matter the country of origin. Riders from Mexico, from Argentina, from Venezuela, were all Panamanians. It simplified matters.

In the jockeys' room Humberto Gracia quickly got out of his silks, and, seated on the bench facing his locker, breathing unevenly, occasionally gasping, he grabbed for iced tea that had lost its ice. He could take in no more than a sip or two (some jockeys only moisten their lips), since any appreciable amount could influence his weight. As a consequence, he and other riders who deal regularly with a weight problem live in a perpetual state of dehydration. Menotte Aristone, who was riding at the time at Liberty Bell, once shared a secret on the rigors of directing a thousand-pound animal in the heat of competition on a liquidless stomach by revealing that he often, in the closing seconds of a race, underwent the convulsions of dry heaves.

"Coming around the turn for home," Humberto Gracia said, "this is where the race is won or lost. If you can cut in and stay in close along the rail, you save maybe four lengths. I always like the inside." He said Memo Gracida had taught him how to switch-ride. You pass the whip by way of the mouth so as always to have one hand on the reins. Humberto Gracia wiped himself off with a towel. A valet, meaning to be funny, asked him if it were true that the Latin Americans, like himself, had it ten times over the Americans, like Walter Blum. "I tell you this," Humberto Gracia said, "I know what I do on a horse is the best anybody can do." He was very serious.

Chapter 8

The sun gave way to clouds, and there was the threat of rain. The crowd moved with the horses. The horses, for the second race, were being led around the walking ring. When the horses were marched through the tunnel, the bettors followed, first placing their bets. They leaned against the rail, the experts looking for telltale signs of lameness, giving forth such opinions as, "I can't bet that horse, he's all bandaged up."

The true expert, of course, never handicaps bandages. Bandages, usually, are nothing more than protective measures, used primarily to guard against scuffing the fetlocks. Some horses wear bandages — cold water compresses — to tighten the sinews, only as far as the paddock; once there, the bandages are removed. Some horses run in bandages. It makes no difference either way. Bettors who let themselves be swayed by bandages are the joke of the backstretch.

With the first race over, some of the giddiness had gone out of the crowd. Now there were more losers than winners. The grandstand losers, separated from the clubhouse richies by the rail that ran from the paddock, around the walking circle, to the tunnel, were already in good voice, bellowing heartfelt wishes of doom to the jockeys who were now getting ready to mount for the second race, which Blum was sitting out. "Imparato, you son of a bitch, break a leg!"

The crowd within the clubhouse — the ladies and gentlemen — were markedly different. The ladies wore hats and fanned themselves gently with their programs. The gentlemen wore jackets, a requirement — so much so that when a guard was seen chasing a pickpocket, handcuffing him, grabbing him by the collar, a lady in the dark as to the nature of the crime was heard to ask: "What happened? Didn't he have a jacket?"

Steadily, while the horses for the second race made their way through the tunnel, the crowd streamed into the building. The two dollar bettors rushed to the two dollar windows, the fifty dollar bettors ambled over to the fifty dollar windows, downstairs and upstairs, some to watch the race perched high above, behind a glass enclosure, seated before a table set with drinks and steak.

Left behind were the groupies — dressed, mostly, in tight sweaters, hot pants, high heels — always smiling the smile of never-to-be-revealed secrets. They knew things nobody else knew, and they would never tell. They used the interim to exchange red-faced whispers with some of the jockeys who, for one reason or another, sat out the race.

A few jockeys took advantage of this inactive period to step outside the jockeys' room for the simple task of sorting out disquieting thoughts. John Mallano, for one, had reason to ponder.

Not so long ago John Mallano had ridden with the best. He rode with Pincay, Cordero, Baeza, Vasquez, Velasquez, Ron Turcotte. He'd beaten them too, enough times to be leading apprentice in New York. He won over a hundred races in New York. Winning over a hundred races in New York brought him respect; being only eighteen, he was all future. The mounts came easily. The trainers practically waited in line. The newspapers in New York ran numerous features on this curly-haired, eighteen-year-old apprentice out of the Bronx who was burning up the track. He was the hometown boy making good in the biggest town of all. He was the American beating the Latins in the game they were making their own. He was youth showing up experience. Then he lost his bug and won all of three races in three months.

The first of these months was spent in New York, a spell with enough rejections to rattle any man's confidence. The trainers who had so eagerly sought his services only days before were suddenly busy — going back to journeymen jockeys of established abilities or breaking in new boys.

"They lost faith in me," John Mallano said with a shrug. "Soon as I lost the bug, nobody would touch me."

Though he was reluctant to admit it, the word was that even the trainer to whom he was under contract had lost faith in him.

"You can't do no good unless people go along with you," he said. "They got to stick with you. Look at Bracciale. After he lost the bug he went about sixty races before he win. But he was getting the horses. He was getting the horses, the good horses, all the time. That's the way he broke out. Now look at him.

"So I left New York," he said. "I was doing no good. Couldn't get any mounts."

The hot apprentice, now without his bug, turned cold.

"I don't know," he said. "I'm as good now as I was before. I don't do anything different. I haven't changed. I don't know what I'm going to do. I guess I'll stick around for as long as I can and see what happens. Maybe I'll get lucky."

He spoke without bitterness. It was too early to be bitter. What's more, the Monmouth meeting was still young, and there was plenty of time to get going again. Very often one hot horse is all it takes: Bobby Ussery, for example, on Lover John. Bobby Ussery, once a leading New York jockey, was unable to get any mounts in New York after returning from a period of settling certain "personal problems." So he went to Liberty Bell, clicked on a horse called Lover John, and had been unstoppable since. Now he divided his time between Monmouth and Liberty Bell.

On the other hand, Bobby Ussery was not a jockey who had to prove his worth without the bug.

The unseen crowd let out a roar, marking the completion of the second race. Soon they would be drifting back.

Chapter 9

Along the backstretch the horses that would run in the third race were being prepared.

In the afternoon there is no quieter, more peaceful place than the backstretch. At Monmouth, as you make your way past the clubhouse stands, you walk some 400 yards on the dirt horse path, shaded on both sides by low-hanging trees and tall, evenly trimmed shrubs. Behind you are the noise and the jostling. Nothing breaks the silence now but the clippety clop of horses going to the races, or coming back — the horses going out stepping high, full of unused run, the horses coming back, sagged and puffing. The sound of the twigs breaking under your feet is firm and summery. With the firehouse straight ahead, to the right is the shed row that houses Shecky Greene, known to his hands as Raggedy Ann. Farther down the right, near the very entrance to the barn area, where the guards check for passes and solicit tips, is the shed row of Royal and Regal.

In the firehouse the firemen and neighboring horsemen, those who have no work to do, sit around the television set, in turn following the changing odds and watching the races. Post time you can hear, though faintly, the starting gate doors clang open and shut, and you can hear the assistant starters shouting instructions to the mounted jockeys and to one another: "Hold 'im right there, like that, that's the way, now you got it, hold, hold, hold, hold, wait, wait, wait, shit, come on, come on, get 'im in, get 'im in, all right take 'im out, take 'im out, watch, watch, take 'im around again, okay, okay I got 'im, three in? I got the two. Two's in. Get the four. Hold it with the four. Six, six, hold up. Nice and easy now. Nice and easy. Hold it with the four. I said hold it with the four. Now, now, now you got 'im. Everybody in? Everybody in? Okay, okay. Let's go!" Then the bell, and they're off.

The trainers are all out front, dressed in their finest, mixing with the clubhouse crowd. Those who have horses in the race wait for their horses to be led out: in the paddock, they take charge of the saddling. As far as they are concerned, the work has been done. Along the shed rows, the grooms are in control.

"He's feeling real good," said Pete Mikos of Hows The King. Hows The King was being given a final brushing. Lynn Dwyer, a hotwalker, was holding him by the shank. "We want you to look real nice and pretty when you get out there," Pete Mikos said to Hows The King.

"How much time we got?" Pete asked somebody.

"Ten minutes."

Aloysius was studying the *Daily Racing Form*. He was said to be a handicapper without equal. He did not like to admit that he bet, but he did. Sometimes, to hide the fact, he wore sunglasses to the windows. To make him feel good, nobody recognized him.

"I don't know if he's going to win," said Aloysius. "You never know with maidens."

Shorty said that with Blum on, there was better than a good chance.

"Blum's going to win number 3,996 on this horse," Pete said. "Whoosh!"

"You never know with maidens," Aloysius said.

"Look at that," Pete said, stepping back in admiration. "He's all dappled out. Fit as can be."

Lou Goldberg said, "I think Blum likes this horse. Last time he bring him in second."

"By seven," said Aloysius.

"He's going to win today," said Lou Goldberg. "You know Blum's got to be trying. He wants them 4,000 wins."

"What does he need 4,000 wins for?" Pete said. "He's got all the money in the world."

"He's a helluva rider," said Shorty. "He's six lengths better than anybody around any day, next to Michael Hole."

"I like Barrera," said Pete. "He's good."

Good as he was, Barrera was having a so-so meet.

"Hold that shank tighter," Pete said to Lynn. Lynn smiled. She said she was feeling nervous. She was rather new to the backstretch. She had once worked in an office. Her boyfriend was studying to become a veterinarian. Track veterinarians can make as much as 200 thousand dollars a year.

"Like you say," said Shorty, although nobody said, "Blum's about the best. Next to Michael Hole. That's right." He was, as always, chewing on a strip of hay. "And that ain't taking anything away from him. Like you say, I remember a horse he win on a time back, he win by twelve lengths. Another boy had been on that horse a dozen times before. Couldn't do a thing with him. Blum get on him, and he win by twelve lengths."

In the jockeys' room, Walter Blum was putting on his silks. He'd sat out the second race — lounging about the swimming pool that was accessible through the back door of the jockeys' room, open only to jockeys and a newsman or two. He was tanned, and there was no doubt that here was a man accustomed to success. Though he'd been leading rider in the country in 1963 and 1964, this was developing into his best year ever. He was winning a high percentage of races, and earlier he had been a threat to win the Kentucky Derby. Whereas in years past three-year-olds of Kentucky Derby quality had eluded him, except in four cases, this spring he practically had his choice among Royal and Regal, Mr. Prospector, and Shecky Greene. In Kentucky Derby preps he had won on all three. As it turned out, he came in eighth on Royal and Regal in the Derby, and Royal and Regal was never the same again.

Walter Blum finished the spring at Garden State, all the while drawing assignments on the finest mounts in the East, not the least of which was Icecapade. Taking it all together, his victories in major stakes, his consistency over the years, his advance toward the exclusive circle of 4,000 wins, Walter Blum was quite simply the premier thoroughbred rider of the day.

The year before, however, Walter Blum had been doing so poorly, in Atlantic City, that one owner was willing to pay money just so Walter Blum didn't get on his horse. Dave Hart, Blum's agent, now sitting back in one of the easy chairs outside the jockeys' room, remembered the story well:

"We went about fifty-nine races before he even won a race. I don't know. You get into slumps. That meet Tejeira went forty-eight races before he win. Nobody said a word. Kallai went about fifty-two races. The same way. Nobody said a word. But Blum! One fellow picked it up in the paper. He'd write, 'Blum is ought for forty-two. Blum is ought for forty-six.' When they do that it puts a little pressure on you.

"Well, one day we rode a horse for a fellow. Bold Etage. He won first time Walter rode him. Next time he rode he got beat in a photo. And the next time he had him in, Walter was in the slump.

"The fellow who trains him is a friend of mine, Jimmy Toner. So Toner told me, he said, 'We got this horse in for Friday. Can you ride him?' I said okay. So Wednesday, the man that owned him, P. Q. Wilson, said to Toner, 'Who you riding on that horse?' He says Blum. Well now, when Blum won on the horse he had his arm around him, and he hugged him, and he was gonna buy Blum this and do that for him. He was a great guy and everything.

"So now all of a sudden, the owner says to Toner, he says, 'Listen, let's put somebody else on him. Blum's in the slump.' So Toner says, 'Well, gee, how can you do that,' he says. 'This kid went out on the horse. That's like slapping him in the face.'

"He says, 'Look, I own the horse. You train him. I pay the bills. I don't want Blum on him.' Toner says, 'Well, I already entered him, and I put Blum on him.' Wilson says, 'Well, somebody told me that you can pay a double jock mount and put another rider on.'

"So Toner called me up, and he told me that the owner wanted to put somebody else on him. So I said, 'Well, is it all right with you, Jimmy, if I go in and see the stewards, and try and stay on him?' He says, 'Sure, go ahead.'

"So I went in and seen Mr. Daingerfield, and I told him what happened. He said, 'Dave, we don't like to do that. We don't like to let people do it. But,' he says, 'it's their prerogative. If they want to take you off a horse and pay the double jock fee, you have to let them do it.'

"So I thought, okay. But see what happens when you turn it around the other way? If I did it to him. If I gave him a call on Bold Etage, and I went to him and I said, 'Look, I don't want to ride this horse. I want to ride Joe Brown in the same race. He's a better mount.' I can't do it. The stewards won't let me off the horse. I'm binded to his call. So it's a little unfair.

"Well anyway, when Walter came into the jocks' room and he saw he wasn't on that horse, he turned red, white, and blue. He got sick. So I walked in, in the first race, and I see him standing outside the jocks' room. He was riding in the second race.

"So I said, 'What are you doing out here, Walter?' He says, 'Dave, you know, when I walked into the jocks' room and I seen that guy took me off that horse — you know last night you told me he might take me off that horse — I got a lump in my throat. I couldn't even swallow.' Walter said, 'I didn't think this guy would do a thing like that.' I said, 'Well, what are you waiting here for?'

"He says, 'Well, the owner comes in here and sits by these benches, and I just want to see him. I just want to talk to him.'

"And here he comes. So Walter walked over to him, and he said, 'Mr. Wilson, what ever made you take me off that horse? Why would you do a thing like that to me?' Wilson says, 'I don't know, Walter.' He says, 'I just don't know.'

"Walter says, 'Well, how could you possibly do this to me? I won on this horse and you told me what kind of a great guy I was, and what kind of a great rider I was and as long as you had horses, I could ride them '

"So Wilson says, 'I don't know. But there'll be other times. I'll put you on him some other time.'

"So Walter says, 'Well, he'll win today.' Wilson says, 'Oh, I don't think he'll win.'

"So Walter says, 'I hope not.'

"Then Walter turned around and walked away. He didn't say anything nasty or out of line to him, you know, but he had to say something. Horse won, too. Tejeira was on him."

According to Hart, the confrontation with Wilson was the closest Blum ever came to losing his cool.

"I'll tell you," he said. "Of all the riders that I've ever worked for, and I've worked for some pretty good riders, he's the real pro. Like Willie Mays. Or Mickey Mantle. He reeks with class. Everything he does he does with class. This is the truth.

"The main thing about Walter, Walter can ride. Walter, I think, if he wanted to ride five more years, or if he wanted to ride ten more years, he could do it. Because he keeps himself fit. And I'll tell you, with him I feel more at ease than with any riders I ever had. Because if he has a good day, and if he has a bad day, he shows the same. I never seen him mad or anything.

"And even when he hit that slump in Atlantic City, he used to try and cool *me* out every night I'd see him. I'd say, 'Well, we'll win a couple tomorrow.' He'd say, 'Yeah, don't let it get you down. We'll be all right. We'll be all right.'

"He's got the right attitude about things. If there ever was a pro, he's a pro.

"The only time I ever got mad through the whole thing, that slump, was one day some guy was standing out in front and he yelled at him; 'Blum,' he said, 'you should only get cancer.' You know, I was sick when the guy said that."

Chapter 10

When they brought out Hows The King, Danny Perlsweig began the saddling, heaping on the horse's back, in quick, nervous motions, the saddle towel, the cloth, the pommel pad, the saddle, and making sure that the girth was tight, just so. Then the bridle, and a tug at the stirrups. Danny Perlsweig worked fast, no matter what he did.

Some of the jockeys were already out, flexing their whips. The alert ones come out early to size up the competition, and the clever, experienced ones get to know at a furtive glance what kind of race each horse in contention will run. The horse favoring a right foreleg will obviously be lugging in left, making it a good idea to stay on the outside of him. The horse favoring a left foreleg will be bearing out, so you will want to keep inside of him. In either case, you will want to avoid close quarters.

Certain things tell you what is wrong with a horse. The horse having trouble with a foreleg tends to nod his head when applying the least amount of pressure to the foreleg. Each step on the sore leg is accompanied by a nod of the head. The horse having a problem with a hindleg tends to rear his head each time he steps on the leg.

Then you have to distinguish between the horses acting up on account of fitness and the horses acting up on account of fear. Bulging eyeballs are one sure sign of fear, and quick side glances and jerky movements at the approach of a human are another. Likewise a sweaty horse usually is a scared horse; a horse with a bright, glossy coat is usually fit — and only a seasoned horseman can tell the difference.

In the paddock Walter Blum greeted Danny Perlsweig with a hug. Then he looked out in the direction of the crowd, squinting, ignoring questions pertaining to the race, and parrying wise remarks with a cocky, contemptuous smile, formed many years ago in the tough streets of Brooklyn.

In the walking circle the jockeys shook hands with the owners and took instructions from the trainers. With the command "Get your riders up!" the jockeys mounted, Manuel Cedeno on Dot's Prize, David Zambrana on Table Turner, Michael Hole on Run Benny Run, William Bromley on Run Yusel Run, Miguel A. Rivera on Prince Gerome, Joseph Imparato on Amavex, Vincent Bracciale, Jr., on Wheeling, Kevin Daly on Tootsie Wootsie, and Walter Blum on Hows The King.

Pete Mikos, Shorty, and Aloysius would watch the race from the grandstand and Danny Perlsweig from the clubhouse. The bettors who had come to know one trainer from another would follow behind at a discreet distance to see how much Danny Perlsweig bet, if he bet at all.

Trainers, of course, do bet, often large sums, and not for the sheer adventure or pleasure of it: for the simple purpose of staying in business. When it comes to that, the trainer who bets on his horse is often too nervous to do the saddling. If the groom likewise has a bet going, the horse will have to saddle himself.

Hows The King, Walter Blum getting him off in his usual pumping style, broke well, squaring himself quickly behind Tootsie Wootsie, who was setting the pace. Leaving the back-stretch, Hows The King extended himself with even, sure strides and overtook the leader. Blum, now in front, whipped left and right, to open up from the oncoming Prince Gerome. In the stretch Amavex began closing but went wide; Table Turner and Dot's Prize made bids but fell back; Prince Gerome came on with a strong, willing rush to finish second behind Hows The King, who won by three lengths.

"Like I said," said Pete Mikos. "Whoosh!"

As usual, more tickets were flung to the ground than cashed. Isaias Martinez had the job of sweeping them up. For that he had a broom, a pan, and a uniform. A tag sewn above the breast pocket advised that the uniform and Isaias Martinez were the property of "Monmouth Park."

In the mornings Isaias Martinez exercised horses for Larry Jennings, a trainer known for his compassion for horses, his gentlemanly ways, his good looks, and his patience in breaking in new help. In the afternoons Isaias Martinez swept.

He did not always sweep. Sometimes he would bend over to inspect a ticket to see if it was a winning ticket discarded by accident, mindful that though these accidents happened none too often they still happened often enough. In this business of dealing with persons who fluctuate from frenzy to despair in the matter of a second, nothing can be taken for granted. Some bettors, so accustomed to losing that even a winning race brings on a mood of deflation, hold on to the losing tickets and let go of the winners, to make complete fools of themselves at the cashier windows. Sometimes, trash cans are overturned, and tickets torn beyond recognition are patched up to form a complete digit.

Isaias Martinez would sweep up all the garbage, never, really, exerting too much effort, always just busy enough to look busy. A sweep here, a sweep there, a glance up at the board, a pause to examine the horses, the riders, the trainers coming out of the tunnel. Apart from sweeping, his most important job was to keep out of people's way. Above all he was not to interfere with the flow of things. That he did well. He was no bother at all, inconspicuous. Unless you were looking for him, you never noticed him.

The Mexican riders were his friends — at least he knew them — and when they were close enough, he'd say something to them in Spanish. Sometimes they would answer. When the race started,

Isaias Martinez forgot the sweeping altogether, engrossed in the manner in which the riders were riding their horses, contemplating their shortcomings. They all made mistakes. Humberto Gracia, though Mexican, made as many mistakes as anybody. He did not have it. He did not have it in the hands. Isaias Martinez would not volunteer this type of information, but if asked, he would tell. He observed all the riders, and they all made mistakes.

Of course in Mexico, going back ten years, Martinez also had made mistakes. He was never the perfect rider, but he was good and effective enough to be well known inside Mexico, riding at the Hipodromo-de-las-Americas with the generation that preceded Humberto Gracia's — the generation of Ycaza. Martinez came to America, leaving behind a wife and four kids, soon after word of Ycaza's exploits reached Mexico. As for his family, he sent money.

Now he could not return. He was sending back money all right, as much as one could on wages. But he could not return because, one, he had a heavy investment going in terms of years and, two, the big time was in his blood, even if his part in it was only from the sidelines.

Isaias Martinez had one serious defect as a rider trying to make it in the States. He never learned English.

Chapter 11

They now wondered if Walter Blum could win the next one and make it two in a row. The sun was out again, making everything clear and bright. The girls seemed more beautiful when the sun was shining, and Monmouth Park had more than its fair share of beautiful girls. In the administration building the agents huddled to compare notes and the latest gossip. The younger agents were forever scribbling something in a notepad. The older ones did not need a notepad. They could make arrangements with a dozen trainers and never have to write a thing down. It was all up there in the head. They were an interesting breed, jockeys' agents. Henry Block, one of the good riders, once said: "Everybody hates the agent, but a jockey has got to have him. He's the bullshit artist. He's the intervene between you and your mistakes."

Robyn Smith was seen making her way to her dressing room. She was in from New York to ride the sixth race on a mount called Lightning Lucy. Robyn Smith was the leading female rider in the country; to most racing fans she would always be "that broad."

For the fourth race of the day, Walter Blum was on another front-runner, the filly Exclusive Sun. Walter Blum had a way with front-runners. He was by far the best gate man in the business, and, what's more, once he got out in front, if he had any kind of horse under him, he was almost impossible to catch. The secret was that in pumping away as he did, he gave the appearance of going all out, when, in truth, he was setting a false pace, always saving enough horse for a strong finish.

In the gate you have to outsmart the horse. You surely can't outfight him. He has to have his four feet firmly on the ground, and his head looking straight down the racetrack. If the horse does that, when those doors open, man, he's gone. By the time the doors are fully opened, he's out of the gate by a length.

However, if his head is cocked to the right, he's going to come out that way, and you're not going to be able to let him run away from the gate evenly. You're going to have to pull him straight, straighten him up, and when you do that you hamper him.

So what's most important is to have his four feet on the ground, coming straight away. A lot of times you can do this, because the horse is calm and nice in the gate. But 90 percent of the horses are not calm and nice in the gate; they're anxious, they're up off their feet. They know what's going on, too. They know that that door is going to open pretty soon and they're going to have to get out of there. So they're anxious, and they might look this way and that way. The horse gets distracted easily. He sees the starter handling another horse next to him, and he'll want to do nothing but look at that starter.

For the majority of horses that's the pitfall — leaving the gate. They're not ready for it. The jockey, no matter how hard he tries to get the horse ready, sometimes he just can't. That horse weighs a thousand pounds. The jockey weighs a hundred pounds. If the horse wants to turn his head, he turns his head. And you're in trouble.

So the best thing to do, I've found, is just to be as calm and as quiet as you can on a horse when he's in the gate, and try to get him to relax. If you relax on him, he'll relax under you. As soon as you tighten up on him, he tightens up under you. They feel this through your body.

That's why you find a lot of girls around the racetrack lately, working horses. They have a light touch, which they transmit to the horse — which is very important in riding horses. You have to transmit some kind of touch to them, so that they know you know what you're doing, without trying to overpower them.

So when I walk in the gate, I try to relax so my horse will relax, and if he does, I can usually get him on his feet looking straight away, and every time he does, he breaks good. But another thing that's important is the horse's mane. When you go in the gate, you should have two hands on the reins and a fingerful of mane, or a handful of mane. When the horse lunges out of the gate, you should come away on the mane, because as he lunges forward the momentum pushes you back, so when it does you are hanging onto the mane. If you come out on his mouth, he'll come away gagging.

Once you've got him breaking away from the gate, in stride, you have to make sure he's going straight. You can't go out or in because you'll bother somebody. After you've got him on his feet and in stride, then it's all according to what you want to do. If you want to take him back, you just ease him back, behind the other horses. If you don't want to take him back, you just reach up and take a nice snug hold of him so that he'll just go along on his own courage. You're not asking him to run. He's just doing what he can do easily.

Then you maintain that position until you get around the turn, until you turn for home, and you try to pick the best part of the racetrack. On a particular day the inside might not be the place to be, so you stay off the inside. You have to know where the best part of the racetrack is. A lot of times all over is good. So you can take him to the fence to save ground. If you're in front, you take him where you can take him. Sometimes you want to go out, but you can't go out. Somebody's got you locked in. Or you want to go inside and you can't because there are two horses in front of you.

When your horse swings around the turn and straightens away for home, that's when you start to ask him to run. If you feel like you've got a lot of horse you wait a little longer. It's according to the horse, too. The horse may want to run. If you sit there too long with him he may not want to run when you want him to run. They're funny that way.

The charts indicated that Exclusive Sun, Blum's mount in the fourth, had a stubborn tendency to quit. In her last race, Blum up, she had finished eighth, thirteen lengths behind the leader, after having set the early pace.

This time, however, there was no falling back. Watching the race through binoculars, focusing on Blum, you viewed a rider at the height of his powers, who knew exactly what he was doing, who did what he did smoothly, efficiently, and with authority, always in total command of his mount. For the initial urging from the gate — with the expulsion "Yaaaah" — the hands were high, flailing away. Gradually, the horse now collected and in stride, both rider and horse in rhythm as one, the hands were lowered, tugging lightly but firmly at the reins, knowing by feel the amount of pressure to apply on the bit.

Holding a secure lead, Blum moved his mount to the center of the track, letting out the reins inch by inch to give the horse her head and let her run at her own will. Into the stretch, he continued hand-riding her, showing her the whip once, as a reminder. For the final dash the hands were raised again, the reins drawn in, the butt higher and higher, pumping, pumping.

Passing the finish line Walter Blum turned his head, looked over his shoulder, and saw what he and everybody else already knew — that he had won, comfortably. The experience, the skill, showed again, too, as, while some riders were fighting their mounts to a stop, Walter Blum let his come to a gradual halt, letting her run herself out. Throughout it all, including the canter back to the winner's circle, there had been no sudden or abrupt moves. Everything was accomplished with certainty and polish.

In the winner's circle Walter Blum smiled for Jim Raftery and his camera, while the railbirds, particularly those on the grandstand side, were having their say:

"Blum, you bum, you did it to me again!"

"Attaway, Walter!"

"Three to go, Walter!"

A few bettors wondered out loud why it was that Walter Blum chose to win only when they did not bet him. "When I bet him, he lose. When I don't bet him, he win. He's murder, the guy." Every racegoer, it seemed, had a personal stake in Walter Blum, at least those who had been around a number of years. Some remembered the thousands of races he had won for them. Others could not forget the thousands of races he had lost for them. In either case he belonged to them, the same way an issue of stock belonged to an investor.

Jim Raftery was in a very good mood. "He's going to do it today," he said. "Today or tomorrow."

Chapter 12

With the fifth race coming up, a sizable crowd stretched out along the paddock rail. Now there was a sense of special excitement among the onlookers. True, the motivating factor behind coming to the racetrack is to win money, but if in the process you stand to witness a moment in history (no matter how inconsequential in relation to things that really count), your payoff can be measured in terms quite beyond dollars and cents. Today, or tomorrow, or sometime soon, Walter Blum would be the sixth American rider to have reached 4,000 wins. Ahead of him were Bill Shoemaker, Johnny Longden, Eddie Arcaro, Steve Brooks, and Bill Hartack. Only Shoemaker and Hartack were still riding. And Hartack, with 4,232, Arcaro, with 4,779, and Brooks, with 4,447, were definitely within reach.

It would be fatuous to suggest that Walter Blum and his quest for 4,000 were of uppermost concern. Race fans had few heroes. They venerated a horse every now and then, the likes of Mr. Correlation and, of course, Secretariat. In years past the mention of, say, Kelso, Carry Back, Citation, Swaps, or a Dr. Fager was enough to fill the stands, for the sheer spectacle. But jockeys, as a group, are regarded as little more than accessories. They enjoy nothing near the adulation tendered athletes of most any other sport. To many race fans, especially those who take infrequent trips to the track, a particular jockey is remembered and forgotten in the span of one race to the next. The explanation perhaps is simple: considering that it is the horse that does all the running, there is no way of being sure how much credit the jockey deserves. The only time a jockey can be certain of having his worth evaluated is when he loses. It was not, for example, Ron Turcotte who won the Triple Crown, but Secretariat. Secretariat, however, in the minds of many, did not lose the Whitney; Ron Turcotte did.

Occasionally a jockey will rise above the ranks and become the subject of awed attention. In New York they worship Braulio Baeza. They worship Braulio Baeza everywhere, and that's taking in hard-nosed, jaded, backstretch horsemen as well. On his visits to Monmouth, the paddock area is usually crammed with horsemen vying for a glimpse of the great Panamanian, and just watching him mount makes more than one horseman's day.

Baeza, several times the country's leading money rider, is the complete professional. In the walking ring, while other jockeys are being sociable, Braulio Baeza will have nothing to do with the formalities of shaking hands and trading quips with the owners (who expect a certain amount of ingratiating attention for their money). Standing gaunt, impassive, haughty, he concentrates totally on the job ahead.

As a rider, he is a workman of precision. Physically (except on a horse) he is no standout. If you met him in the jockeys' room before being introduced, you might mistake him for a custodian. No sharp, black eyes — common among most Latin riders — no thick, black hair, or smooth, well-cared-for, near-brown skin. His cheeks are deeply inverted; his complexion almost sallow. But there *is* something about the way he carries himself — a calm, quiet, self-assured bearing — that sets him apart, that lets you know that this is no custodian. He appears to study you through half-open eyes and perhaps wonders why anyone cares enough about him to talk to him. The height of immodesty? No, soon you understand: to a man who works his craft so finely, so close to the marrow, discussion is superfluous. Racing horses is no game; it is a job, a job that calls for maximum focus on detail and respect for the resourcefulness of its craftsmen. Idle talk, conjecture, betting, fans, newspapermen, all these are beside the point. The horse matters, the rider matters, the race matters, and that is all.

Not far behind Baeza in esteem are Pincay, Velasquez, and Vasquez — all of them Panamanians.

Then there is the American, Walter Blum. His rise to prominence has been steady rather than spectacular. He was born and raised in Brooklyn. His father drove a delivery truck for the *New York Times*. "We were close-knit," Walter remembers, "warm, not rich or even comfortable. Just ordinary. My dad always worked. He met his need just as well as he could. We never wanted for anything, but we never had the things that rich people had. We did the best we could."

Walter's formal education came to a stop with the completion of his sophomore year in high school. During that year, when Walter was sixteen, Tony Falco, a classmate, induced him to pay a visit to Jamaica Racetrack, where the previous summer Falco had worked as an exercise boy. From that point, it was only a question of bringing his parents around. "They didn't like the idea at all. They weren't familiar with racing, or racetracks, and what they did know about the racetrack was 'bad.' " They also wanted him to finish school. Finally, though, they acceded. "They knew I wasn't much of a scholar."

His first move was to try to get a job with the legendary Hirsch Jacobs. But Jacobs had all the help he needed. So Walter canvassed around, looking for a job as a jockey. He thought that was all there was to it. You presented yourself to a trainer and said, "Hi. Here I am. I'll be your jockey." Frank Cundal finally gave him a job.

"Here's my pony," he said. "Take care of him and start mucking out his stall."

Mucking out his stall?

"What does mucking mean?" Walter asked.

Cundal showed him. You took the pitchfork, see, and you cleaned out the manure.

Walter did this for a month and a half. He also walked hots. Later he groomed. In fact, he did everything but get *on* a horse. On May 2, 1951, Walter again approached Hirsch Jacobs. Jacobs was the man everyone wanted to work for. Year after year he was leading trainer in the state — in the country. Some said he had a patent on it. He had a shed row of some forty horses, most of them claimers — horses virtually no one wanted. He claimed them cheap — he did not believe in putting out too much money for a horse — and improved on practically every horse he claimed, sometimes dramatically. In the forties his horse Stymie retired with earnings of $918,485, coming that close to being the sport's first equine millionaire. Even today only a little over a dozen horses have won more. Stymie had been claimed for $1,500.

Jacobs was a private man, religious and superstitious. He neither smoked nor drank, and he frowned on betting. (Blum: "He was like a saint. He was a real clean-living guy. He wouldn't say shit if he had a mouthful.") Supposedly he had a superstition about brooms. The origin of it was unclear, but according to racetrack lore, the sight of a broom in his barn drove him to near apoplexy. Henry Block tells the story of one stablehand who, in revenge for a sudden firing, littered the length of Jacob's shed row with brooms. "He was not amused," remembers Block.

Persons who smoked, drank, or carried on were not welcome in Hirsch Jacobs' barn. A man's shed row, after all, was his place of business, and if respect was to be shown anywhere, it was to be shown in the place that was the source of his income. In the Jewish teaching, *parnosoh* (livelihood) was a sacrosanct endeavor. Jacobs was particularly outraged by those who had the audacity to smoke in his barn. "Please, do not smoke in my barn," was the message he gave anyone who did, stablehand and owner alike. The threat of fire was of secondary importance. The impertinence of it was what mattered most.

Jacobs was a man of fixed principles. He was extremely successful, so the burden of acquiescence was yours. If you wanted to work for him, you had to abide by his rules. If you did, perhaps there was a future for you.

"Be here tomorrow morning," Jacobs told Blum.

That made it May 3, 1951. Two years later, to the day, Walter Blum rode his first race — he lost. In the interim, he learned. "Jacobs taught me everything. Everything that I learned, I learned from him. How to get along with horses, how to handle horses, how to gallop horses, how to work horses, break horses from the gate — everything about horses that he could possibly teach me in two years he did. He never rode a horse in his life, but he could tell you how to ride one. After I had worked for Jacobs for a couple of months you couldn't take me away from racing for anything. I loved it then, and I love it now. I worked at it, and I was at the racetrack all the time. When we were done in the morning a lot of guys would go home. Well, I would go have lunch, and I'd go back to the track and watch the horses break from the gate, watch how the jockeys warmed them up, watch the actual races being run, and watch the actual races through the stretch when they came to the finish to see what they did. There were some good riders you could watch, like Eddie Arcaro. Ted Atkinson. When I did ride my first race, at Jamaica, I felt I knew what I was doing."

He broke his maiden July 29, 1953, astride Tuscania. He was eighteen years old. About a year later the association with Jacobs came to an end. The parting was not especially amicable, coming about after misunderstanding had turned into some bitterness. Jacobs had more than the one barn. In fact, he had horses spread out all across the country, and the jockey who rode for Jacobs was expected to lead a peripatetic existence. Blum preferred staying in one place. So he asked Jacobs for his contract. "When I did, he got a little mad at me. He felt, 'Well, I got you started, and now you don't need me anymore, so you're going to leave.' He said, 'I'm not going to let you leave just like that. I don't want you to think you're going to go away for nothing, just because you want to go. If you want to go, you can go. If you want to pay for your contract, you can pay for it.' "

Jacobs asked $2,500 for the contract. He did not want the money for himself; he did not need it. He was simply making a point. Walter made out a check for $1,000 to the school Jacobs' son was attending. The remainder went to B'nai Brith.

Chapter 13

In the jockeys' room, Carlos Barrera, who would be riding Highty Tighty in the fifth, playfully slapped Walter Blum across the knees with a towel. In front of his locker, getting into his silks, Barrera said, "He is one of the toughest riders to ride against, that Blum."

Barrera's valet was inserting lead in Barrera's saddle pads to meet the race's 117-pound weight requirement. Barrera had a weight problem in reverse. He did not weigh enough. He did about 105. There were a thousand jockeys who would give up anything short of their lives to change places with Barrera, with respect to weight. Never having to undergo the sweatbox, never having to flip, and being able to drink all the water he wanted showed. Barrera was one of the few riders you ever saw with round, rosy, red cheeks and cheerful eyes. A certain tightness in the face, a certain hollow look from the eyes, which you saw in other riders, who were in the throes of starvation and dehydration or on a diet of appetite-curbing drugs, you never saw in Carlos Barrera. He was baby-faced. The girls said he was cute. He was particularly cute in Mexico, where he was leading rider every year from 1963 to 1967. In the States, where he started riding at the end of 1967, he did all right, too.

He'd already won over a thousand races. The year before, at Monmouth, he won three stakes. The same year he won the United Nations, in Atlantic City, aboard Acclimatization, beating out Dubassoff and Red Reality, in the record-equaling time of 1:54 for the mile and three sixteenths. Flit-to, carrying 110, the lightest weight ever for the United Nations, set the record time in 1967, ahead of Assagai and Fort Marcy. A year later Dr. Fager won the United Nations carrying the highest weight ever — 134. Braulio Baeza rode him. Blum won the United Nations in 1965 aboard Parka, and Parka was named National Grass Course Champion of the year, as were most horses that won the United Nations.

"I like this country," said Barrera. He spoke in a high-pitched voice, his manner altogether pleasing. "You work hard, yes. You are working a whole day. You have to be at the track the whole day. And is tough. You have a lot of competition. You have a lot of jockeys from different places. And you have to keep busy all the time. Keep working. Working in the mornings. Two or three horses in the mornings. In the afternoon you have to keep winning races all the time. But you make a lot of money. You live good. You have a nice living. Sometimes I send money home."

In the hallway, getting ready to step out, were Humberto Gracia, Michael Hole, Buck Thornburg, Carlos Lopez, Paul Cespedes, Joseph Imparato, Walter Blum, and Carlos Barrera. There is always, at this time, a knot in the stomach, a fear that is never discussed. Walter Blum was the first to step out. He smiled at a few people. He winked at a couple of pretty girls.

At the very corner of the paddock, a valet named Joe was admiring a painting. "Oh, that's beautiful," he said.

The painting was of horses, in a race.

"I think the yellow one is going to win," said the artist, a woman from England.

Joe bought the painting for some two hundred dollars, then called over a few of his valet friends and told them how beautiful it was. They said the painting was beautiful.

"Looks like the yellow one's going to win," one of them said.

"Yes, I suppose I did have a preference for the yellow one," said the woman from England. She was going back in a few days.

"If you want her to paint a picture for you, better tell her now," Joe said to a friend. "She can mail it to you."

"Can you paint me a picture of a jockey?"

"Yes, I possibly could, but at the moment I'm doing strictly horses."

"Do you do portraits?"

"Yes, of horses."

"Isn't it beautiful?" Joe said, holding up his new possession.

"I mean can you paint a portrait of a jockey on a horse?"

"Yes, I can, but I do prefer to stay with horses."

"You like horses."

"Oh, indeed."

"They're beautiful animals, all right," said Joe's friend. "Nobody appreciates the beauty of them."

"That's true, and it's a shame."

An eavesdropping fan said, "The yellow one going to win?"

"I believe so."

"He seems to be ahead."

"Ever so slightly."

Joe said, of his painting, "Isn't it beautiful?"

Joe had served some ten years under a trainer who, he claimed, had never given him a break. A jockey was what he'd always wanted to be.

Somebody spotted Carlos Barrera — still standing by the entrance — and yelled out, "This one's yours, Barrera. No way you can lose, eh, Carlos? No way you're going to let Blum make it three in a row."

Another fan yelled out, "You need this one, Carlos. One more and you got him."

Barrera needed one more win to match Blum in the standings for this meeting. Barrera was, at the moment, fourth in the standings, with 36 firsts, 34 seconds, and 28 thirds, out of 257 mounts. Walter Blum, in third place, had so far recorded 37 firsts, 32 seconds, and 21 thirds, out of 203 mounts. (In second place was Michael Hole; 45 firsts, 36 seconds, and 31 thirds, out of 231 mounts. Bracciale was the leading rider with 47 firsts, 58 seconds, and 37 thirds, out of 309 mounts.)

Barrera, for some reason, rarely drew the attention of vindictive hecklers, perhaps on account of his colorless riding style. He was not a flashy rider. He was good with the whip and had no qualms about hugging the rail. He was adept at coming off the pace and competent in getting to the front.

He did the job.

Pete Mikos, who observed riders carefully for the day he would become a trainer, felt Barrera did more. In fact, he liked Barrera over Blum. He called him an honest rider you could always rely on to put forth a thorough effort. Blum felt much the same way about Barrera. His agent didn't. "I think he's just a very ordinary rider," Dave Hart once said of Barrera. "I think Blum could go to sleep and outride a jock like Barrera."

The year Blum was having his slump in Atlantic City, Barrera finished leading rider.

A man and woman were sitting by a table on the terrace. The woman said that when Barrera had first come to this country, he had lived with them. The man said there was no finer gentleman than Barrera. They had come down to watch him race. The woman asked her husband if he'd as yet had a chance to talk to Barrera. He'd just come back from the paddock, her husband had. Yes, he said, Barrera was going to have dinner with them. Oh, that's wonderful, said the woman. They decided, however, to stay on the terrace and not watch the race.

Chapter 14

Charlie Dewer was a Blum man. "I don't bet the horses," he said. "I play the boy." Charlie Dewer was a regular. He was one of the faces you always saw. When you went to Garden, to Atlantic City, to Monmouth, you always saw the same faces, and one of the faces you always saw was Charlie Dewer's. He had played Blum in the third and had been right. He had played Blum in the fourth and had been right. Now he was playing Blum in the fifth. "Got to be," he said. "Blum. Speed. Got to be."

He had not as yet placed his bet. The horses were now being paraded in front of the stands: about ten minutes to post. Charlie Dewer, following a twenty-year ritual, first went to the john. In the john he nodded to the attendant. The attendant, though he did not know Charlie Dewer by name, nodded back and said, "Seat?" Charlie Dewer said, "No." The attendant said, "Towel?" That would mean at least a quarter. Charlie Dewer said, "Okay." Before a race, Charlie Dewer was usually on the generous side, not expansively so — anymore — but just enough to placate the gods of fortune. Once, before a race, he had tipped a bathroom attendant five dollars, for no particular reason. His horse won.

For a time after that, Charlie Dewer was throwing five dollar bills around to anyone who looked like a bathroom attendant. If there was no bathroom attendant in sight, he went searching for one. He dropped the habit when it began to show no return.

In the bathroom, he washed his hands and wiped them with the clean cloth towel. "Thank you," said the attendant. Then Charlie Dewer made his way to the two-dollar exacta window and played the four/three ten times. The four, of course, was Full Allowance, Blum up. The three, Buck and Wing, Hole up. Then Charlie Dewer went back to the john.

"Seat?" the attendant said.

"No."

"Towel?"

"I already had a towel."

Charlie Dewer would visit the john two more times before the race.

Standing on his seat out front, adjusting his field glasses, as the horses went postward, he said, "They say Blum can't win three in a row. He's hot, let me tell you. When Blum's hot, he's hot. I remember at Garden. He was so hot you couldn't touch him with a ten-foot pole. Look, he's the best there is. He's one of the tops. When they're like that they can win three in a row, four in a row, five in a row, makes no difference. He's in a league by himself.

"Look, the guy's gonna win 4,000 races. What's he short? Three? You got to be tops to do that. My wife, you know, she don't like me going to the track. But when it's Blum, she always wants me to put two dollars on him for her. I remember one time at Garden, I was in the john, and some guy said, he said, 'You hear Blum got shot in the head?' You know, I really believed it. I didn't ask around. I didn't want to spread no rumors, you know. So I went home, and I asked the wife, 'You hear anything about Blum got shot in the head?' 'No,' she says. So I turn on the radio. Nothing. I turn on the television. Nothing. I figure that's a big thing. Should be somewhere. Turns out to be a crank, you know. One of those cranks. But you had to believe it for a while.

"A guy like Blum, there's always people out gunning for him. They bet him heavy and when he lose, who knows? Nuts, there's nuts all over. He's so good, see, that some people bet him all the time, and when you bet a guy all the time, now you know no matter how good the guy is, you know, he's going to lose more than he win. Natural. I mean you take a baseball player. Even a baseball player that hits .300, it means he misses seven out of ten times. Know what I mean?

"Me, you see, I don't bet Blum all the time. Just most of the time. When I figure he's got a shot. I always say, 'When in doubt, bet Blum.' I mean when there's no other horse a standout, you got to go with Blum. Like this race. You got to go for Blum. Take a look. July 11 the horse come in third, running close to the front all the way. Who was on him? Cedeno. Blum's got to be an improvement. Last two races before, the horse come in third and second with Gracia. Now Gracia's a good boy. No getting around that. But he ain't no Blum. Not yet."

Charlie Dewer began breathing very fast when the horses left the gate.

"He's way back," Charlie Dewer said, looking out through his field glasses. "That's no good. If Blum ain't in the front right away, that's no good. That number six, who that number six? Yeah, Move a Native. He's running. I was afraid of that. I knew I shoulda played that horse. I was worried about that horse. He's out there by three lengths, that six. No, nobody going to catch that six. I was thinking of playing that six on top. Look at that three. Hole, right? Yeah, that three giving him a race. That's how it's gonna be, the six and the three. I was gonna play it that way. I shoulda played it that way."

Into the stretch it was still the number six, Move a Native, and the three, Buck and Wing. Carlos Barrera's Highty Tighty had got off to a poor start, having gone wide in the backstretch. Now in the stretch he was making a bid, but it would be short.

"Hey, hey, hey," shouted Charlie Dewer. "Blum's making a move. Blum's making his move."

Move a Native fell back.

"Sure," said Charlie Dewer. "Figured. That six was sure to quit. That's why I didn't play him. I shoulda played the three/six.

But Blum was still coming on. He was moving between horses.

Now he had only the three to beat.

"Blum's coming on, Blum's coming on, Blum's coming on!"

The race finished four/three; Full Allowance (Blum) and Buck and Wing (Hole). Charlie Dewer was very pleased. "They say Blum don't come from off the pace," he said. He was counting the ten tickets he had on the four/three. When the result was announced as official, Charlie Dewer said, "Three in a row for that Blum!" and rushed back to watch the replay. He was trembling all over from the excitement, though, really, there had never been any doubt.

Walter Blum got his picture taken in the winner's circle for the 3,998th time (and for the last time that afternoon; he finished out of the money in his two other appearances). But there would be no horse in the picture. It had come back lame.

Robyn Smith came in first in the sixth race but had the win taken away from her for interference. Walking back to the dressing room, through the tunnel, she was seen crying.

Chapter 15

Steve Brooks had already won his 4,000, and more. He was one of the handful.

Steve Brooks was saying, "I rode some darn good horses in my time. I rode Round Table. I rode . . . ah . . . it ain't easy remembering. I rode so many. I won the Kentucky Derby in 1949, on Ponder. Yeah, I won the Kentucky Derby. Nineteen forty-nine. I think it was 1949. Yeah, it was 1949. There's nothing like being in the Kentucky Derby, and I mean just being in it, not the winning. You don't think about winning the Kentucky Derby. Hell, that's just a dream. Hell, when people meet you, you know, and they know you're a rider, they don't ask you nothing except were you ever in the Kentucky Derby. It's the finest thing that can happen to a rider. It's like I say, it's a dream. You're in a daze, and you can't believe it's happening to you. Why, I remember, I remember that day, when I was coming around for home. Why, when I come around for the homestretch I suddenly realize, it hit me, hey, I'm on my way to winning the Kentucky Derby! Why, soon as I crossed the finish line, why, I jumped off my horse, I was so excited and all, and broke an ankle. Yeah, broke an ankle."

That year, 1949, Steve Brooks led the nation's riders in money earned.

Steve Brooks now worked for the trainer Harold Tinker, at Liberty Bell. He exercised horses and was something of an assistant. You reached Harold Tinker's barn by walking up a slight knoll. It was the first barn in a series that extended right and straight ahead. When you looked out, you had a view of the track, the grandstand, and the back end of the jockeys' room.

Steve Brooks had been cleaning a saddle when the visitor asked to talk to him. He'd been lathering the saddle and his hands were wet. He apologized for not being able to shake hands. He was surprised that someone had sought him out for an interview. It had been a while. Since his retirement a couple of years ago, he'd settled into the serene if unglamorous life of the backstretch, mixing among the hands as one of them, expecting no special attention for having once shared the limelight with Eddie Arcaro and the rest. Many of the younger hands, including a few who worked for Harold Tinker, knew him as "Mr. Brooks." He was simply an old man who knew his way around horses. His history had already been written — the record book sealed — and no one knew that better than Steve Brooks, though accepting the fact had been a hard lesson.

That in his career as a rider he had won 4,447 races was meaningless — now. Now it was a number. In the heat of it, it had meant much, and Steve Brooks had been a man of importance. His advice had been followed, his opinions sought, and his words written down. Now he was forgotten, and all that remained were the memories and the scars and the broken bones, which were about all they left an old jock.

Lathering the saddle, he told the visitor to come back in an hour, after which time he would be cleaned up. An hour later Steve Brooks apologized again for not having been able to shake hands. Here was a man who had once known his way around millionaires, who had once had a fortune of his own, and it was important for him that one knew that. Class was not something that came and went, like everything else. He had changed into a clean rodeo-style shirt and crisp jeans. His boots glistened from a recent shine.

Seated on a bench cooled by a tree, he looked down at the puffing horses cantering back from their works. Below, a car drove past every now and then, leaving behind a cloud of dust. It was late morning, the jockeys were arriving to report in, and a few of them could be seen making their way into the jocks' room, through the back, screen door.

There, stepping out of his car, was Don MacBeth, the Canadian, who a few days earlier had been thrown off a lame horse along the stretch and who, to ease the dying horse's pain, had run out midfield to bring it back some grass.

Farther down you had a view of the grandstand, silent and empty except for the debris — wrappers, cigar and cigarette butts, beer containers — that the workmen would take their time cleaning up, all of which helped form the conclusion that Liberty Bell was a most graceless setting for thoroughbred racing. Someday soon the move would be made to Neshaminy; meanwhile, Liberty Bell was an embarrassment. The barn area itself, with its broken-down, unpainted barns and its howling dogs, making most shed rows unapproachable, was a study in contrast to Monmouth's. As a track it had major league status, but jockeys who had a choice stayed away from it as much as possible, and horsemen on the way up preferred the pastoral settings of the New Jersey and New York tracks. But when you were in need of work, and not quite on your way up, any place was good enough.

"Best horse I ever rode," said Steve Brooks, "was Citation. Some people'll tell you he was the greatest horse ever. He was a great horse all right, but Secretariat is the greatest horse that ever run. Ain't never been anything like him. Big strong horse, that Secretariat. Biggest horse I ever saw. Citation, he was pretty much average size. But he was one fine animal. He could do anything, that horse — he could win up front, he could win from behind, anything. Had a lot of heart.

"Like I says, I rode some pretty fair horses in my time, but not too many like Citation. You don't get too many horses like that. A rider is lucky if he gets one in a lifetime. Yessir. Most of your riders, they ride the ordinary horses. Common stuff. To get to the good horses, the real good horses, you got to be good, yeah, but you also got to be lucky. Most of the horses you get to ride, you ride 'em, and you forget about 'em. Hell, I can't remember every race I rode. I can't remember most of the horses. I been riding some forty-odd years, and you get to see a lot of horses in that time. I rode every racetrack in the country. Some of them, some of the racetracks, why they've since been torn down. Office buildings gone up in their place.

"Most of the horses you ride never get to amount to much, but you got to ride 'em every day. You ride 'em every day and if you're lucky, why, one day you get that good one, and it makes it all worthwhile. Not that you're wasting your time with the common ones. You ride enough of those, and win on enough of 'em, you're gonna make money. But for your pride, it's nice to get that champion horse."

Steve Brooks stared down at his boots and wiggled an ankle a few times as if trying to shake off pain. He brought the ankle up to where he could reach it without bending over and rubbed it. He crossed his right leg over the left one and rubbed the kneecaps of both. Then he crossed his left leg over his right leg.

"I rode Citation as a two-year-old," he said. "I didn't ride him when he won the Triple Crown. That was Eddie Arcaro. But I rode him after that again and we won some big races. I won the Hollywood Gold Cup on him."

Citation collected $100,000 for winning the Hollywood Gold Cup: July 14, 1951. That amount put him over the million-dollar mark, making Citation racing's first equine millionaire and Steve Brooks the first jockey ever to ride a millionaire horse.

"I knew when I won, when I crossed the finish line, that I was bringing home the first million-dollar horse," Steve Brooks said. "But it didn't mean too much to me at the time. As I recall, I was mainly worried about the race. The papers made a big thing out of it, and there was a lot of talk about it, but, I don't know . . . it didn't mean too much to me at the time."

Money, in general, did not mean too much. That's usually how it is when it's coming in fast, so fast you think there's no end. When it stops, that's when it takes on meaning. By then it's too late.

"I made good money," Steve Brooks said. "I made real good

money. Lost it all. Bookkeepers, you know."

The injuries too were a bad break.

"I was pretty lucky for the longest time," he said. "Never got hurt, never real bad. But later . . ."

Later came the broken collar bones, the dislocated shoulders, the busted kneecaps, the cracked elbows, injuries over and over again to the joints that could take no more — all coming about so quick in succession that finally the sum total had to be seen for what it was, age. He retired at forty-nine.

Giving it up had not been easy, especially for a man who had not been careful with his money and knew how to do one thing only. Out in western Nebraska, he'd started riding when he was four. His father was a horse trader, and the two, father and son, would go from town to town, state to state, buying and selling horses — and back home, before he could read, Steve Brooks was breaking them in. Horses, that was all he knew.

When he came of age, he started riding for money, riding the small, crummy, cheap, out-of-the-way tracks. "They educated you," Steve Brooks said. "Why, the riders in those days, they were big. Real big. Big, hefty fellows. Farm boys, most of 'em were. They could as soon ride an ox as a horse. I was the smallest rider there was, and they knew it. Why, two of 'em would ride up along side you and lift up your horse, just like that. That's right. They'd just come at you from both sides and lift your horse up off the ground. Nothing you could do. They could do as they wanted. Lot of times they'd take to whipping you, whipping you across the back, sometimes across the face, all the way around. Come back to the jocks' room all bleeding and bruised up. They'd beat shit out of you in the jocks' room, too. Wasn't much of a jocks' room in those days and you were pretty much on your own and you had to fight 'em every inch of the way. Mean — they were mean. They were mean all right. Why, they'd Sunday you every chance they'd get. They'd grab hold of your reins and lead you around the track like you was a baby. They'd just grab hold of those reins and lead you around. You try and fight back, they shove you off your horse. That's why it didn't pay to be small in those days. They'd grab you and they'd push you and enough times I never made it to the finish.

I'd be off my horse somewheres along the backstretch. Had to walk back, too. Then they'd be waiting for you in the jocks' room.

"That's how it was. There were no cameras around, no patrol judges, so you could do pretty much as you pleased and if you were big enough you could get away with murder. Sure, quite a few riders got killed. I come close plenty of times. You pull a man off his horse, you know, and he's down on the ground, horse comes up behind him, runs over him, and that's it. And I ain't talking about no accident. I mean they'd run over you on purpose. No telling what they'd do. You had to win to eat. That's the only way you could eat, was to win. You didn't win, you didn't eat. You starved. So when it come to a choice they'd as soon run over you as kill a fly. They educated you. I got educated. I got educated all right. I got educated good. I learned to get away from the gate real fast. Later when I rode the big tracks I got the reputation for being fast away from the gate and good with the whip. Well, that come about from being educated. I taught myself to get away fast so's nobody could catch me."

Steve Brooks got up off the bench and began walking. The morning work phase was coming to an end. The horses were now in their stalls, having been fed and treated. A groom, here and there, could be seen raking the walkway.

Outside one shed row, a young hand wearing a cowboy hat was spit-polishing his boots. Along another shed row a fat girl was being pinched in the behind. She said, "Ouch, stop that!" The fellow who had pinched her said, "Now, you know you like it," and laughed. Most of the girls seem to be on the heavy side. Some of them are college girls, working their way through the summer; some, not. They all dress the same, so you can't tell the difference, even in the way they talk.

The horsemen, excepting trainers and jockeys, reside on the grounds, living in apartment units that have, in some cases, air conditioners and, in all cases, television sets. This is where they eat, where they shower, where they sleep, and where they live. They are — the men and the women — happy people. They get up early in the morning, they work hard, but they always have something to look forward to. They certainly are not lonely people.

They have each other, and they have their horses. The horses hold them together. For all they are concerned, the outside world is another planet — wars, the stock market, political scandals all pass them by without touching them. The newspapers are always turned to the racing page.

"Later on," Steve Brooks said, "I learned pacing, and got to being good at keeping my horse one or two off the lead so's to have something left over at the end." He did most of his riding around Chicago — Sportsman's Park, Arlington — and got to making it big when he hooked up with Calumet Farms. That's when he started making a name for himself. But the years riding the small, crummy tracks had hurt him. People remembered him as a rider who came from second-class company. So it was a matter of his proving that he could ride first-rate horses against first-rate riders as well as lame horses against farm boys, tough though they were.

Steve Brooks strolled back to the bench under the tree and sat down.

"The horses today are better," he said. "They're also worse. They run 'em so much I don't know how most of 'em can stand on their feet. They keep running 'em over and over again, makes no difference if they're sore or what. I don't see how they can do it, the horses."

Steve Brooks shifted the weight of his body from one side to the next. If not in pain, he was in some discomfort. He rubbed his eyes from the dust the wind had blown up. Down below horse vans were pulling up. The guards pointed the drivers to different directions. The area around the jockeys' room was becoming active. To the left, beyond the hedge, sprinkler trucks were watering the track, a peaceful sound. The dogs were still howling, here and there, and in the overall quiet you could hear laughter from a certain direction.

"Mr. Brooks?" the girl said. She had come up from behind. "Do you want us to take out that colt?"

"Be right there," he said.

The girl went away, and he sat for a few moments in silence. Then he said he had no regrets, but wished he hadn't got injured.

That's all. It was surprising how the injuries had come — all at once. Now he could not raise his left arm level to his shoulder. That injury more than the rest, or perhaps combined with the rest, had incapacitated him as a rider.

Even with the serious injuries he had taken on mounts, against the advice of doctors and his better judgment. He rode them to pay bills. He rode them because he knew that once a rider stopped riding, there was not much else waiting.

"I can still ride," he said. "I'm in good shape and I'm fit. Except, you know, for my left arm. Can't do nothing with it." He tried raising it, to show how he couldn't. "Won't go," he said. "Except for that, I can still do everything. But if I had to left hand a horse I couldn't."

There were trainers around, he said, who would still give him mounts. Certainly he was fifty-one, but the age itself was not the factor. The left arm, that was the factor. Couldn't left hand a horse if he had to. So that's why he wasn't riding. Wouldn't be fair.

Someday perhaps he would ride again. That left arm. Just might heal.

Thursday Morning

Chapter 16

The Monmouth Queen Diner, located on Route 35 about a hundred yards from a very active military post, Fort Monmouth, and about two miles from Monmouth Park, which is right off Route 36, the main highway, is one of several hangouts favored by horsemen and horseplayers. At night the Monmouth Queen replays all nine races of the day on a television set in the dining room. In the morning the Monmouth Queen is a source for the *Daily Racing Form.*

This early in the morning — around 6:30 — is an especially pleasing time at the Monmouth Queen Diner. The breeze from the ocean is still in the air and a man can sit and have his coffee in peace, read his racing paper, which came out last night, and slowly, painstakingly, make his selections for the afternoon, occasionally sitting back to enjoy that flush of warmth that comes to a man when he knows he has found something in the words that will elude the others — a joy matched only by, say, a scholar who has finally come to terms with a particularly elusive passage of the Scriptures.

This early in the morning a man can feel serene and peaceful and know that maybe this afternoon will be the afternoon to win every race he bets on. There is nothing that says that it has to be otherwise, not this early in the morning.

In the Monmouth Queen Diner the horsemen from Monmouth — the trainers, the jockeys, the grooms, the hotwalkers, the pony boys, the clockers, who are tired of taking their breakfast break in the track kitchen — start coming in around eight and take over the place with their smell and talk of horses and of people who work with horses. They — the jockeys especially — talk only among themselves and regard the most casual nod of a stranger as an intrusion. (Jockeys, because of their size, know quickly enough who belongs to them and who doesn't.) They tell jokes that are funny only to them and stories that have been told over and over again. Most of the time jockeys sit with jockeys, trainers with trainers, grooms with grooms, and girls who work on the track with other girls who work on the track. A very pretty girl, or a girl with masculine ways, sometimes sits with the men, but then the conversation is not the same.

When the jockeys sit together in a booth, they are loud and foulmouthed, but at the approach of a trainer they are respectful, more relaxed and discursive here than in the work-setting of the backstretch, but still respectful, checking the temptation to complete the dirty joke in progress.

As a group, horsemen bring with them wherever they go an air of excitement that is contagious. The racetrack, with its demands, its deadlines, its opportunities, its challenges, gives its men and women a sense of purpose not to be found in any other kind of work. There is that horse that will finally break its maiden and finally make money for its trainer, fulfill the sentimental wish of its groom, and snap the rider out of his season-long slump. There is nothing to equal the exhilaration of preparing for the next race, and horsemen are forever in a state of preparation — always looking ahead.

So they often are loud and sometimes crude.

But at 6:30 in the morning the Monmouth Queen is still quiet, serving no more than three or four customers at the counter, obviously horseplayers. The horseplayer is not necessarily the man in the filthy T-shirt guzzling his beer and smelling of grease. He can be the meticulous accountant who draws satisfaction from working with figures or the RCA engineer to whom the *Daily Racing Form* charts are a challenging puzzle, especially with money on the line. Or he can be a man who looks like an accountant or an engineer but actually has dedicated his life to beating the horses.

He wore a checkered beige suit and was sitting on a stool near the edge of the counter. He was sipping coffee and smoking a Corona.

He had a *Daily Racing Form* in his lap. It had already been worked over.

"You a horseplayer?" he said.

"Sometimes."

"I mean do you play the horses?"

"Sometimes."

"Well, I play the horses. All the time. I'm a professional horse-player." He said this matter-of-factly. "I been a professional horse-player all my life. Ever since I left the Navy in 1947."

"You make a living?"

"Yeah I make a living. I sent two daughters through college. My wife ain't starving. No thanks to the system, mind you. See if you was a horseplayer, I mean an everyday horseplayer, I would ask you a question."

"Let's say I am."

Through the smoke of his cigar, he regarded the few people in the diner with suspicion. Then he smiled.

"See, I'm looking to form an organization of horseplayers. A sort of union, you might say, to keep watchdog over the people who run the races. If you're a professional horseplayer like I am you know as well as I do that a lot of these races ain't exactly on the up and up, if you get what I mean."

"They're not?"

He chuckled.

"You think I'm kidding you, huh? You take a look sometimes and see how these jockeys stiff their horses. You watch the instant replays?"

"Sometimes."

"Well ya ain't gonna get nothing out of watching the instant replays. The only way you can see what's really going on in a race is from that straightaway shot that the stewards use. What you see in the clubhouse is the view from the top. You don't really get to see what's going on. That's the question. Why shouldn't the horseplayers get that angle too. What are they trying to hide from us?"

"I don't know."

"I'll tell you what. They're trying to hide all kind of monkey business. That's why I want to form an organization of horseplayers. If we get enough people we can go to court and make them install a television that gives the straightaway shot. That would eliminate a lot of the monkey business, I can guarantee you that. I would also like to go to court and subpoena all the straightaway films from the past few years. Myself I can't do it. I already been mixed up with the law."

"In what way?"

"Are you kidding? See sometimes I tout . . ."

"Isn't that illegal?"

"It shouldn't be. It's unconstitutional, I mean them pulling you in for touting. There's no law on the books says you can't tout. Know what I mean? When I tout I don't do nothing that ain't within the law. I mean I don't set nobody up. I got real information."

"How do you get this information?"

"I got ways."

"How do you pass on this information?"

"I got regular people. Hey wait a minute! I ain't one of *Them* touts. You know, the kind that sets people up. I work strictly alone."

"How is it if you don't?"

"You mean those guys that work in pairs? Well, I'll tell ya. See, one of them picks a mark, see, and he just stands himself next to his mark and he sort of casually strikes up a conversation and he points to a guy by the rail, his partner, you know, and he says to the mark, 'Gee, you see that guy up front? That guy win the last three races in a row. I seen him collect. I don't know how he does it. He must know somebody.' So now the mark's interested. See, he's set up. Then he walks away, this guy who set him up. So now the other guy that was by the rail sort of ambles over to the mark, you know. Like he's just passing the time of day, he says something like, 'Nice weather we're having.' The mark says, 'Yeah. Say, I hear you been doing all right for yourself.' The guy says, 'Yeah, lucky I guess.' The mark says, 'Say, you like anybody in this next race?' So now, see, the guy says, 'Yeah, well, I got the horse in the next race.' The mark says, 'You do?' The guy says, 'Sure, no doubt about it. Listen, if you want I'll put a hundred dollar bet on the horse for you. You give me a hundred bucks and I'll make the bet.' And that's it."

"What happens to the hundred bucks?"

"Depends. Some touts make the bet and if the horse win, they take a percentage. If the horse lose, you don't want to see that guy again. Some touts don't make the bet. They take the money and run."

"What happens if they run into this mark again?"

"Well, see, these here touts, they know everybody around the racetrack. They know everybody in every racetrack around the whole country. They likewise know the other touts. They got kind of a network. Yeah. One time in California they even had a convention. So anyway, they got everybody spotted. They know the people. They know the guys that been around and them they don't touch. They know the guys that come for once and them they hit. They don't pick on nobody they know there's a chance they'll see again."

"What happens when they do see him again?"

"Then there's trouble. A tout'll say, 'Hey, here's your money. I been looking all over for you.' But it don't always work that way. Some of these suckers really get worked up, and they point the guy out to the security officers. Don't talk to me about these security guys."

"Why not?"

"They harass the life out of you. They harassed me all the way from New York to California. They got their network too. They ruled me off New York. They ruled me off California. They got no cause to rule me off. I'm a professional horseplayer, and I make my living playing the horses. One time they got me on a loitering charge. You believe that? I had 265 bucks in my wallet. Loitering. They wanted to know how I come by the money. I told them I won it at the racetrack. They pulled me into court, and I spent a night in jail. See, they find out you're a professional horseplayer and right away they think there's something shady about you. Now I never done nothing illegal in my life. I only want to be left alone to do my business. It's tough enough as it is, let me tell you. I mean you got to fight the odds, and you got to fight the monkey business. That's why I say we should form an organization and fight back."

He asked for his check and on his way to paying it, he said, "Think about it."

Chapter 17

This morning the entrance to the backstretch was backed up with cars, each passenger waiting his turn to present the guard in the booth with his identification. Usually the wallet identification was sufficient, but this morning the barn area was undergoing a "Security Check" so a rear view mirror sticker also had to be visible.

It was now about seven o'clock and already uncomfortably warm. The backsiders meeting the security requirements, or known to the guards by face or by car, were waved by and sent off with a smile or a kind word. Others sometimes were stopped and questioned; and a few were turned back. Some visitors who were refused admittance took their case to the higher-ups in the nearby security building.

A girl of about nineteen, in jeans and a sweat shirt, stood near the security building, waiting to be announced. "Girl up front looking for work," a voice blared over the loudspeaker. Sometimes there were job openings. They would also give a capsule review of her life. "Experienced hotwalker up front," they would say. Or "Inexperienced hotwalker up front," as was the case. She said her name was Sandy, from Maine, and she was broke. Standing a few feet away from Sandy was a boy of about sixteen who had already been announced and was now waiting for someone, anyone, to claim him. He was looking for work as an exercise boy, though he'd never been on a horse in his life, except on a merry-go-round. His ambition was to be a jockey, and he was in a hurry because he was still growing. "I hope I don't grow no more," he said.

Upon entering the barn area the first shed row on the left was Jimmy Croll's, but Jimmy Croll was busy watching Walter Blum on the Today show. Walter Blum and Ron Turcotte were being interviewed by Gene Shalit. Ron Turcotte talked about Secretariat. Walter Blum talked about approaching 4,000 wins. Gene Shalit reminded his audience that Walter Blum was two shy of 4,000, and that he could reach that magic number this afternoon.

While Jimmy Croll was watching television, his workers were being checked for identification cards. The police, most of them agents of the Thoroughbred Racing Protective Bureau, zigzagged from barn to barn, stopping everybody in sight. They frightened a lot of people, especially those who were on the grounds illegally, but those who were here illegally were already in hiding, having been forewarned by the grapevine or by that certain smell in the wind.

The TRPB did its job as well as it could, but it could never rid the backstretch of all undesirables, who usually fell into three categories: illegal aliens, criminals (men and women with police records), and drug pushers. (The drug pushers were the newest and most worrisome problem.)

The illegal aliens are notably difficult to weed out. They get a job with a trainer sympathetic to them, or with a trainer who saves money by employing persons who are in no position to bargain, forgo the requisite fingerprinting, and practically never leave the grounds, thereby avoiding a check on their credentials. They live this way from backstretch to backstretch, coming out in the open only when it is time to move on to another track — but even then they hide in the vans. Security checks, like the one this morning, are capricious — surprise being the best form of attack — but the illegals are a nimble group, having mastered the technique of staying a pace ahead or a step behind the police. Some, of course, are caught.

Jimmy Croll returned to his shed row when the Walter Blum - Ron Turcotte spot on the Today show was over.

Jimmy Croll's wife was thrilled by Walter Blum's performance. "He was so natural and easy-going," she said. "He was perfectly at ease, as though he'd been doing this all his life." She was beaming. "He could have been a big television star." Ron Turcotte, she said, had been on the nervous side. Walter Blum had to cover for him.

"Yeah, Walter really knows how to handle himself," Jimmy Croll said, speaking of him as you would a member of the family, which, in a sense, Walter was, having ridden for him off and on a good number of years. Jimmy Croll had known Walter Blum through some good times and some bad times.

"Last winter in Florida," said Croll, dismissing his wife with a nod, "Walter was doing poorly, and he was hustling for mounts. He was doing no good. He come over to my barn, and he asked me if I had anything for him. He was going from barn to barn, you know? Surprises a lot of people to find out that a top jockey'll have to do that, go from barn to barn. Well, he don't have to do that when he's going good, but when he's going bad, he's just like the rest. A trainer don't care if a rider's won 3,000 or 10,000 in his lifetime. It's: What have you done lately? Anyway, Walter come over to my barn — you know we've been friends through the years and he run some good races for me through the years — and he asked me if I had anything for him. I said, 'No, Walter, I don't.' He said, 'I'm in a slump, I need a break.' So I said, 'Okay, get on this horse, Brazen Brother. He's gonna win.' Blum get on him and he win. I gave him his next seven winners in a row, and he got hot again."

He got very hot. He rode Croll's Royal and Regal to victory in the $130,000 Florida Derby at Gulfstream (assuring him of a spot in the Kentucky Derby), and on Mr. Prospector he broke the track's sprint record, doing the six furlongs in 1:07 4/5 — finishing nine lengths ahead of the field.

There was no forgetting Blum's confidence in himself and Royal and Regal in the heady days following the Florida Derby victory. He was sure that this time he finally had the mount to carry him to first place in the Kentucky Derby. When, moments after he won the Florida Derby, he was asked what he thought his chances were against Secretariat, he said, "Fuck Secretariat!"

"I don't know if going to the Kentucky Derby was a smart idea," Jimmy Croll said. "It takes a hell of a lot out of a horse." It is not easy to understand Jimmy Croll. He speaks rapidly, in sputters, and frequently overshoots his words. "That's not to say the Derby itself and the two other classics are necessarily what wastes a horse — it's those two-year-old races, the preps. One after the other. They ruin the horse."

Across the way, near the firehouse, two security men, who'd just jumped out of their car, were interrogating a man who spoke English with a Spanish accent. The security men stood over him, hands on hips. The frightened foreigner said he had left his identification card at home. Where was home? Home, he said, was someplace. He pointed in the direction of someplace. The guards looked in that direction; then they looked at one another. They could see no home someplace, they said. Where exactly was home? The man started crying.

Jimmy Croll said, "I just did a study on horses that had competed in the Kentucky Derby through the years. The statistics tell the story. Eighty-five percent of them never come back. They were never the same again, and most of them never run again.

"But owners, you see, the owners, they get that fever, that Kentucky Derby fever, and there's no talking to them. When you explain to them that that one race could ruin a horse for good, well, they say, my horse deserves a shot.

"Two times I quit an owner on account of that — because he wanted to be in the Derby and I was against it."

The man who had a home someplace was taken away.

"So after I quit these owners," Jimmy Croll said, "they gave them over to another trainer, and one of them run the horse in the Derby. The horse run in the Derby, and he broke down. Wasn't worth a dime after.

"Wasn't worth a dime even before the Derby. Those two-year-old races and the three-year-old preps took it all. Two-year-olds, they're babies. A horse doesn't reach maturity until he's five. Yet you run them when they're two. Hell, they've just learned how to walk. You can't expect them to run, week in, week out. Sure you can run them, but then you might as well forget about them."

The sun was coming out strong. A hot wind kicked up a shower of dust.

"That's what it is," Jimmy Croll said. "The owners and the trainers. They don't plan ahead. They see that quick money, that instant glory, and they can't wait to rake it all in. Every owner, practically every trainer, has that dream of standing in the winner's circle Kentucky Derby day. I don't know why it means so much, but it does. I think it's a disease.

"This year I had to go with Royal and Regal, my first Derby shot. He'd shown me a lot and the owner wanted him in. He'd won the Florida Derby so convincingly that I couldn't say no. Looking back, I don't think it was worth the heartache."

Royal and Regal almost did not make it to the Derby.

"After all the excitement," Jimmy Croll said, "after all these years you finally look forward to going to the Derby, the night before the race you get this: I was having dinner — sportswriters' dinner — when I get a call that my horse has come up with a swelling on his foot. Well, I rushed over and there it was all right, right on the same spot, over the bar shoe, that had been abscessed before. I can't tell you how upset I was. You couldn't talk to Walter."

Walter Blum spent a sleepless night — as, of course, did Jimmy Croll.

The affected area on the horse's leg was treated with poultices, and the next morning the swelling was down. Ordinarily the horse would not have been asked to run so soon after a problem. It was, however, Kentucky Derby day; officially he was sound; so he ran. No one will ever know how much it took out of him, but the facts do suggest that it may have cost him his future. Same as with Jimmy Croll's Mr. Prospector, who looked, for a while, to be the nation's top sprinter. Had he not been rushed (he was scratched for the Derby but had run in one prep too many), had he been brought along slowly, in Croll's usual manner, there was every possibility he would have gone on to become the greatest sprint champion of all time. Later, on April 20, 1974, Walter Blum up, he broke Garden State's track record for six furlongs, still off his best form. As one awed bystander remarked, "If that horse hadn't got hurt last year, you never would have heard of Secretariat."

For a time, Jimmy Croll had it all. He had two horses that were destined for immortality. Only Lucien Laurin, with Secretariat and Riva Ridge, was considered as fortunate. In fact the two trainers are an interesting study in contrast. At one point they stood as equals. As trainers, each reached an enviable peak at about the same time. Much was made of the fact that the two would clash head-on in the Derby. Some even gave the edge to Croll. Whereas Laurin had only Secretariat, Croll had Royal and Regal *and* Mr. Prospector. But, as it developed, Laurin went on to reach greater heights with his fabled charges, while Croll suffered fall after fall.

Now Mr. Prospector's stall was minus Mr. Prospector. He was on the farm recuperating from a cannon bone fracture. Another horse, one not nearly as good, but healthy, was occupying his space. Royal and Regal was present all right, nibbling away at his feed, but he was in no condition to do any racing.

He had run a few weeks before at Liberty Bell — convincingly out of the money. He had been up against horses that at an earlier day would have wilted at his presence. Croll, at the time, excused the poor showing on the basis of Royal and Regal's still-inflamed coronet. Walter Blum blamed it on another horse, saying that just when he was beginning to make his run around the turn for home, he was clipped from behind. Both excuses were good. When a horse starts going downhill, the excuses are always good.

Now Jimmy Croll walked over to a stall near the end of his shed row. "This is good old Parka," he said. "I brought him along nice and easy and he became one of the greatest grass horses ever. He was grass champion in 1965. Blum rode him." Jimmy Croll patted the horse on the flank. The horse nosed him. Adopting a baby-talk tone of voice, Jimmy Croll said, "Ain't that right, Parka? Yeah, sure."

Jimmy Croll rubbed his palm against Parka's face.

"This is a real sweet horse," he said. "Sweet, gentle disposition. I love him. He's my all-time favorite. He's retired now. He's done his work. Now I want him to enjoy his remaining years. I'll be putting him out soon. Let him romp around. He's been good to me. He's my pet. Aren't you, boy? Yeah, sure you are."

Chapter 18

Dave Hart sat on one of the cement benches in the center of the kitchen compound reading and not reading a newspaper in the one spot not protected from the sun, biding his time for when Walter Blum would return from New York and his much-talked-about appearance on the Today show. Dave Hart had already been in the racing secretary's office with the other agents, nervously listening as the scratches were being shouted out, pleased that none of the mounts his boy was set to ride this afternoon was being scratched. The agents with scratched horses mutter and cuss, especially if the one mount is all they have going for them.

From where Dave Hart sat, the kitchen was to the left, the racing secretary's office to the right, the horseman's lounge straight ahead. Since it was not yet nine o'clock, the horseman's lounge was bare, though soon enough it would be crammed with sweaty bodies, the kitchen had few customers, and the racing secretary's office was servicing a number of agents with overnight entries so that the agents could place, or try to place, their boys on mounts not already spoken for. Dave Hart had no need to contend with these agents. Trainers were coming to him. He could weigh one offer against the other. Dave Hart, the sun reflecting off the bald spot that extended from his forehead, was in an extremely good mood this morning.

He had every reason to be. He was handling the book of one of the very best jocks in the country, and this jock was having the very best of seasons. The money was coming in as fast as the horses. Dave Hart got a 25 percent cut on all of Walter Blum's earnings.

This afternoon his boy was on five mounts, which was just fine with Dave Hart, as any more would do his boy no good, what with Blum now at an age where a long rest between races was necessary, though the way he'd been riding as of late, pacing beautifully, keeping himself out of traffic problems, his timing as sharp as could be, you would hardly guess that this was a jockey going on forty, supposedly closing out his career.

Dave Hart was well aware that the two wins could be achieved this afternoon without much trouble. Blum had the horses. He was to ride Ravenous in the first, Angel Clipper in the second, Good Hand, Danny Perlsweig's fine mount, in the fifth, Hardboot in the ninth, and between the seventh and the eighth, in an exhibition, he was to ride the champion three-year-old, Impecunious.

This exhibition contest was of more than casual interest: it would pit Linda's Chief, considered the supreme three-year-old outside Secretariat, against Impecunious, a colt that had so far amassed close to $190,000 in purses, and in eighteen starts had been out of the money only four times. The third horse in the race was See The Jaguar, but he was already being dismissed as an also-ran.

Michael Hole would ride See The Jaguar, and Braulio Baeza would be in from New York to ride Linda's Chief. So in this race you would be seeing some of the finest riders compete atop some of the finest horses. Blum against Baeza. The great American against the great Panamanian. You also had England well represented in Michael Hole. But since this was to be an exhibition race — no wagering permitted — suppose Walter Blum was to reach his 4,000th win aboard Impecunious — would it count?

But that was for later. Meantime, Dave Hart was taking in the sun. Yes, he admitted, with a broad smile, three times he had turned Blum down — starting back there in 1970 when he was handling the book of Ray Broussard. "Some people have a loyalty to people; some don't." Because he had a loyalty to Broussard, he rejected Walter Blum, who had just split with his agent of seventeen years, Harold Fats Wiscman.

Hart had fond memories of the since-retired Broussard. "Broussard was the greatest money rider there was. When it come to winning a big stakes race, I'd put him over anybody. But he had that weight problem, and that limited him. I used to get mad at him when I worked for him because a lot of Mondays he couldn't make it . . . 'cause over the weekend he'd fill up too much and couldn't make the weight. He could never do lighter than 117 and that wasn't bad, but he was one of those guys if he does 117 today and he eats tonight, tomorrow when he comes into that room he'll weigh 122. So I'd get a little mad at him. But a guy has to eat. So then he'd go into the sweatbox. I used to watch him sweat and take off . . . why, I've seen him take off six, seven, eight pounds in one morning. I'd feel sorry for the guy. It's really tough."

When Hart and Broussard parted company, Blum made another attempt at getting Hart for his agent, but Hart was tied up with another rider.

Finally, in Blum's third attempt, Hart was disengaged, and the two, Hart and Blum, teamed up to form one of racing's most potent combinations. And Hart, who had been an agent for the likes of Ray Broussard and Jacinto Vasquez, was now handling the book of the leading American rider.

The rough road, including that slump in Atlantic City, was past; ahead was a fine afternoon. Soon Walter Blum would be in from New York and together they would go over the afternoon's program and talk about the agenda in store for tomorrow. If Blum got back early enough, perhaps he would exercise a horse or two. If he did not get back early enough, no problem.

"If you're not going good, you have to fight hard to get on horses. You have to struggle. You have to fight harder, and you have to fight everything.

"If you're doing good, it's easier for you."

Dave Hart closed his eyes and let the sun warm his face.

Chapter 19

You would not say Paul DeMarco, Mickey Solomone's agent of only a few days, was having it easy. You would have to say he was struggling. But he was young, and he had unshakable confidence in himself, and in Mickey Solomone, and that was not a bad place from which to start.

At the moment, however, confidence was about all he had (though soon enough, in the Atlantic City meeting to follow, he would guide and see his boy through win after win, to finish the meeting very near the top, behind Walter Blum). In fact, he was searching the kitchen compound for signs of Mickey Solomone.

"Have you seen Mickey?" he said, his light hair windblown.

No.

Mickey was missing all right, and there were trainers waiting and depending on him. And since Mickey was new to Monmouth, the trainers would not wait and depend too much longer. Paul DeMarco said there had to be some justice. Yes, his boy still had morning commitments to fulfill — and that was to the good — but he had already exercised ten horses and a guy deserved a break. A guy deserved a break but go tell that to the trainer who still had horses waiting to be exercised by Mickey Solomone. If he did not meet these commitments, there would be no horses to ride in the afternoons — and word would get around: this boy is unreliable. An agent could not have that. An agent lived on the reputation of his client.

Paul DeMarco began a circle of the compound, which was now coming to life, busy with horsemen and horsewomen all dusty and dirty, many of them heading for the kitchen, some of them just hanging around outside talking and laughing, appreciating jokes peculiar to their subculture.

Near the door of the kitchen was the newsstand. The vender, a man with a sarcastic smile unremittingly smeared on his face, sold the dollar *Racing Form* for a dollar and the 35-cent program for 50 cents.

A horseman obviously new to the backstretch asked the vender for a program.

"Fifty cents," the vender said.

"Forget it, friend."

"Big spender," the vender said.

When Paul DeMarco walked by, the vender nodded toward the parsimonious horseman and said, "Big spender." Paul DeMarco did not smile.

Frank Lovato, having just come from Harvey Rosenblatt's shed row, was relaxing on a bench outside the horseman's lounge. A seventeen-year riding veteran, Lovato was raised in New Mexico on his father's dairy farm. Lovato: "I had to get up four in the morning to milk the cows. The first trainer I went to work for told me, 'You know,' he said, 'if you want to be a jockey you're going to have to get up early in the morning.' I said, 'What do you call early?' He said, 'Oh, around six.' I said, 'Great. That means I'll be able to get in an extra two hours' sleep.' "

Paul DeMarco eventually wound his way back to the compound entrance.

Paul DeMarco was a handsome man. He had blonde hair, and his face always looked as if it had just been scrubbed. He was in his mid-thirties. He wore the sharpest suits, light colored, to match his complexion

"I don't see Mickey any place," he said. "I better find him. I can't have trainers getting mad at us at this point."

At this point, Mickey Solomone was making a fresh start — not his first. He'd just come from Delaware, where he had not exactly been a ball of fire.

Mickey Solomone had been a top rider — on and off: one good year, one bad year. Throughout his career he had been restricted by the nemesis known to sportsmen as attitude. Mickey Solomone did not have the right attitude. He lacked motivation. He was, heaven help us, a thinking person — in a field that, generally, singled out for reward only those gifted with mindless application.

Though he would hardly define it as such, he was in large measure an existentialist. He shrugged his way through life. When he rode well and even when he was in contention for leading-rider honors, it was only a matter of time until he asked himself the question, "So what?" and dropped it all, eventually to absorb himself in books, travel, and girls, to name but three broadening distractions.

The girls came easily for Mickey Solomone, perhaps because he was attractive and an athlete. "Some girls," Mickey Solomone would say, "go wild and really get turned on when they see those white pants." These girls hang around the jocks' room where there are plenty of white pants to choose from, which is not to say that the girls are accessible to every jockey. They invariably make their selections from the top of the program's leading-rider chart. "They get some kinda charge out of doing the big time with a jock making it big; you know, heads turning in restaurants and all. As long as the money is coming in, the broads are around. Then the jock gets cold, he's blown all his money, and she's gone."

Anyway, Mickey Solomone could never be accused of taking racing too seriously. "For some guys," he would say, "racing is everything. Day and night it's racing. I can't go along with that. There must be more to life."

You would not learn much about life in the hotbox or in the jocks' room in general. Henry Block put it this way: "When a rider walks into the jocks' room and he's sixteen and he stays in there for ten years, when he walks out he's still sixteen. There's nothing to learn in there except horses, girls, horse talk, and horseshit."

So mainly for this reason Mickey Solomone took leaves of absence whenever the mood struck him, and consequently, never (at least not yet) met his promise — and a rider of promise he was. He had raw talent and proper instincts, and he had the perfect build — rather tall, lean, and very muscular around the shoulders. He could be compared to Howard Grant, and was. Both had the raw talent and both were thinkers.

Grant, it was generally believed, was the very best rider of all. His trouble was weight. In a recent newspaper interview he'd talked about the misery that attends a jockey; the abstemious existence and the flipping. He noted that at a party, when most people were stuffing and drinking themselves silly, the jockey was fortunate if he could indulge himself in a glass of water. He posed a challenging question: If it were between making a hundred thousand dollars a year and starving, and making a regular salary and eating well, which would you choose?

This article was widely read along the backstretch, particularly among jockeys. It was one of the few times a jockey had been so candid. Most jockeys do not like to discuss these matters and grow especially silent on the subject of flipping. Menotte Aristone, for example, admits privately that flipping is a part of being a jockey, but he is much against publicizing the fact. "Be better if you didn't say anything about that," he says. "Most riders find it embarrassing."

Mickey Solomone has no weight problem. Self-discipline is his problem. When he first came to Monmouth from Delaware, he came very much alone. He had no agent and had just been divorced.

"Mickey and I ran into each other out of the blue," Paul DeMarco said, half his attention focused on the horsemen ambling by. "We knew right away we were going places together, and I've been doing all right for him since.

"I've been getting him on as many mounts as he can handle, at least in the morning."

Paul DeMarco paused to smile at a few passers-by. They were trainers — the ones he smiled at.

"So he's supposed to work a horse for Sacco this morning and I can't find him. I just come from Sacco's barn, and he's asking me where Mickey is. I told him I'd go look for him. I told him Mickey was working all kinds of horses this morning, but he don't want to hear none of that, and I can't say as I blame him. He's not too happy with me right now. I don't know. Sacco's got some good two- and three-year-olds, and I'd really like to get in good with him. Shit, there he is right now."

Sacco was making his way to the kitchen. He was really checking up on Paul DeMarco.

"Hello, sir!" Paul DeMarco was red in the face. Sacco ignored the apology and brushed right past him, into the kitchen.

"Boy, he's hot. He's a bit hot. But what can you do? Mickey's already been on ten horses this morning. You see how hot he was?"

Paul DeMarco's eyes stayed glued on the kitchen door. "I'm not too worried. Mickey and me are gonna be all right. We're gonna be leading rider. I don't care about Blum. I don't care about Bracciale. Mickey, you see, Mickey's the best. I'm not just saying that because I'm his agent.

"See, I've seen a lot of riders and there's nobody like Mickey. Now that he's got himself straightened out he wants to be leading rider and, hell, we're gonna work hard and he's gonna be. See, now he's ready to settle down. He knows he only got a few good years left."

Sacco strolled out of the kitchen with a container of coffee. This time Paul DeMarco let it go.

"We're gonna have some good years together, Mickey and me," Paul DeMarco said. "I finally got the rider. Tom Kelly, you know, the clerk of scales, he told me he never seen a rider as strong as Mickey Solomone. See, Mickey is strong. He's the strongest rider there is. That's no bullshit.

"I used to admire Velasquez. I still do. Velasquez is the fastest man with the whip. He can change whips faster than any rider. That's the way I felt until I saw Mickey. Now I'm convinced Mickey is faster. You'll never see a rider go to both sides faster than Mickey. He really helps a horse — and that's the kind of a rider trainers are looking for. I got him.

"My dream, see, is to be leading rider in New York. First we're gonna make it big here, then we're gonna make it big in Atlantic City, and then we're going to go to Florida and finish leading rider. After that, New York! I got connections in Florida and Mickey knows a lot of people in New York. Right now we're meeting everybody we can, we're making friends, we're making connections, so when we leave we'll be all set up. They'll be waiting for us.

"See, I'm just learning the ropes, but I'm getting better every day. I'm learning. Every day I learn something new.

"Like yesterday I went to see this one trainer and he looked like a cowboy. I thought he was a cowboy. So I talked to him like a cowboy. Then I find out he's from Louisiana, a Cajun. Now you got to talk differently to those people. They like to be babied a bit. So next time I'll know. Next time I see him I'll know how to talk to him. I put him off, I know I did. I wasn't coming on right.

"You can't talk to a Cajun the same way you talk to a cowboy. You can't talk to a trainer from New York the same way you talk to a trainer from Texas. These trainers from New York, you got to talk to them in their language. Now these cowboys, they don't talk much. They just like their boys to work hard."

J. Willard Thompson, in cowboy hat and boots, was heading in the direction of the racing secretary's office.

"I'm gonna be putting you on two horses." he shouted out to Paul DeMarco.

"Thank you, sir."

"Just ride 'em good."

"We will, sir."

Paul DeMarco said, "See there's a guy that knows his business. He's a cowboy, and he's got real class. A real classy guy. Real straight. No bullshitting. He doesn't like to be bullshitted. I learned it the hard way. When I first went to his shed row I really put the pressure on. But I found out that's not the way to do it with him. I tried to buy him a cup of coffee, but he's one of those trainers that don't like to sit around in the kitchen. He likes to be with his horses. Drinks up his coffee real fast and gets back to work. So the next time I saw him I didn't bullshit him and I didn't put the pressure on. I just asked him if he'd give my boy a chance. He said okay, and see, now he's putting us on a couple of horses in a couple of days.

"See," he said, breaking away to have a word with Sacco, who was making another appearance, "I'm learning."

Chapter 20

Walter Blum was back from New York in time to exercise a horse for Herb Paley. Herb Paley had a twenty-horse shed row, located opposite Jimmy Croll's, near the entrance to the barn area. Herb Paley has a face mapped with worry lines. He never smiles, outwardly. His manner is gruff and direct. He started out some seventeen years ago under Sunny Jim Fitzsimmons and has done pretty well for himself. He works hard and is at his shed row every morning by six — every morning for seventeen years. He never takes a vacation. Like most people who never take vacations, he is proud of the fact. The most he takes is an occasional Sunday, when he gets to work by eight instead of six.

Herb Paley has something to show for all this hard work and dedication. He is the state's trainer representative, which puts him in a position of respect, as all persons wishing to become trainers in New Jersey have to pass through him. He gives the tests. Herb Paley also has ulcers to show for his hard work and dedication.

"So you're back," Herb Paley said to Walter Blum.

"Yeah, I'm back."

Herb Paley said he was honored to have such a distinguished television star under his shed row.

The horse Blum was to exercise was being saddled up.

"Come on," Herb Paley said, "I got to go to the racing secretary's office for a minute."

Herb Paley and Walter Blum got into Herb Paley's car. On the back seat, a dog was sleeping. When the dog, which was shaggy and arthritic, was feeling all right, he followed his master around. When he wasn't feeling all right, he would stay in the car, on the back seat, and sleep.

"You got a dog?" Herb Paley said.

"Yeah, I got a cat, too," Walter Blum said. "Funny story about that cat. Happened right here at Monmouth, last year. One morning I'm in my apartment and I hear a scratching at the door. It was raining like hell, so I figured maybe it was the rain. But I still hear the scratching. So I open the door and there's this little cat. I chased it away and went back to reading the paper. But that little cat was still scratching away. So I let it in, toweled it off, fed it, and sent it out again. Okay. So I figure that's that. The next morning, there it is again. That was it — I had me a cat."

Walter Blum then explained why, at first, he had chased the cat away. "I'm allergic to animal hairs," he said.

Walter Blum is allergic to the hairs of all animals. For a man who makes his living riding animals, an allergy to animal hairs is no big help. "There was a time I couldn't get near a horse. I would wheeze and get sick as the devil." There is no cure for the mysterious ailment, but medication keeps it under control.

Walter Blum does not like to talk about his allergy. He is afraid it will hurt his chances of getting mounts. For the same reason, he does not talk much about the fact that he is — has been since the age of two — sightless in the right eye.

Back in Herb Paley's shed row, as Walter Blum was being boosted on the horse, Herb Paley said, "She's rapid. Don't fight her. Let her ride under a mild restraint."

"You want her to benefit from this workout, right?"

"Right."

Walter Blum directed his mount past the gates, onto the main oval. Herb Paley took the dirt road, by foot, on his way to the dugout, from where he would observe the workout. The dugout was situated by the one-eighth pole.

Herb Paley, walking fast, lit a cigarette. He was not having too wonderful a meet. He was a betting man, and he bet on every horse of his he thought had a shot, which was all too frequently. In the afternoons he sometimes said, "I think I got a shot in this race. At least we'll be on the board." When he was not on the board, he would say the horse had had a stumbled start. In the mornings, in the late mornings, Herb Paley plays cards in the horseman's lounge — for big money. He is after big money.

"I always wanted to be rich quick. That's my makeup. In California, years ago, I ran tip sheets. I even ran a dog tip sheet. To me, as a kid of, say, fourteen, there was only one way of looking at it. Money. I was an envious individual. I saw a guy riding around in a big car, boy, I was envious."

He decided, in his early years, that trainers got rich quick.

"I was always interested in horses. As a boy, horses was it. So I started on the tracks in New York — I'm from the Bronx — and the truth of the matter is I even worked for nothing, just so I could get in the inside of it. I was all over the country trying to make this here mythical million dollars. To be a big shot."

Now in the dugout, Herb Paley focused the field glasses on his horse and Walter Blum. There were others on the track as well. One young apprentice was sitting very uneasily on his mount. He was being guided by a pony boy, the pony boy leading the apprentice's mount by the shank.

Walter Blum was getting Paley's horse started for her two-mile gallop. He started the horse off slowly, letting her gradually limber and warm up. By the time she hit the one-eighth pole, she was going strong and smooth and was into her gallop. Herb Paley clicked his stopwatch every time the horse passed a quarter-mile marker. Walter Blum, like any rider of experience, knew to the fraction of a second the time his horse was doing. As the horse progressed around the track, she picked up speed with each stride.

In full run, her rider was down in the seat to keep the leverage off his legs. For the finish, Blum pulled in the reins, bringing the horse to an easy halt.

Herb Paley was pleased with the workout. The time had been good, but time wasn't everything. Most horses, actually, can do the time requested by their riders, if their riders are skilled enough. So a horse that does three furlongs in .38 is not necessarily a horse that can do no better. He has simply been restrained. For this reason the listed workouts in the *Racing Form* are not always the horseplayer's best guide.

Later, in the shed row, Herb Paley would want to know from Walter Blum how well the horse had handled the track. Had she taken a good hold of the surface? Had she grabbed it? Or had she let it slip and get away from her? Then, had the horse traveled sound and good, without any weakness of limbs? Only the rider had this information and in this respect was indispensably valuable to the trainer. The rider, and only the rider, could tell if the horse had traveled smoothly. A horse could make good time but still run as though he had had a flat tire.

Heading back to his shed row, lighting another cigarette, the lines across his forehead grooved deeply, criss-crossing like a network of telephone wires, Herb Paley said, "The tension is always with you in this game."

Herb Paley's specialty, though he had not planned it that way, is cheap claimers. Like so many other trainers who condition cheap horses, Herb Paley lives on the hope that one day he will come upon a horse that will, under his care, "turn the corner," and develop into a champion. Once, some time ago, he had that pleasure. He had claimed a horse called Nadagar for $4,250, a horse that for his previous trainer had run primarily on the dirt, even though he had been out of a fairly decent grass dam. Noting the horse's family, Paley immediately moved him up to $10,000 company, in a grass race, and the horse won in fine style. Paley then moved Nadagar up to stakes competition and was rewarded with some $50,000 in purses in a period of 60 days. "He took to grass like a duck takes to water. That other chap never explored that avenue of racing. A horse, especially a two-year-old of valued pedigree, has got to be exploited. No matter how bad he goes for you, you can't give up on him. You've got to keep training him and exploit every avenue of racing until you find his true pinnacle of achievement or success."

In the hands of one trainer a horse may be a washout. In the hands of another, the horse may develop into something. That is why you keep claiming. Perhaps you would find a quirk the previous trainer overlooked — "a change of equipment, this or that; something ridiculous, like maybe going over the brush, steeplechasing. You don't know what avenue could be the true one." Once he had explored all these avenues and if the horse still lost money, Herb Paley usually resold him. "I don't want to see that horse because to me he's discouraging" — as he is to the owner. A losing horse is a demoralizing presence in a shed row and, after a time, can cause a breach between owner and trainer. Win or lose, in addition to the initial outlay, the owner pays all the bills and taking in blacksmith, veterinary, and vanning services, plus the cost of boarding, the total amounts to something like $30 a day. "Every time you call the owner and tell him the bad news, that his horse lost another race, I don't care how patient you are as an owner, how much bad news can you absorb about the same subject?"

This is where the tension, the ulcers, come in. The tension is not necessarily relieved even with a champion horse. "Here you can have a horse today worth a hundred thousand dollars, he injures himself, breaks a bone, and he ain't worth a dime the next day."

All of which teaches you to be hard. "You can't be sentimental in this game. You got to be pretty callous."

Herb Paley and Walter Blum met and talked for a while outside Herb Paley's tack room, and since it was getting to be around ten, the conversation broke off, with Paley making tracks for the horseman's lounge and Walter Blum heading for his car.

"Paley's a funny guy," Walter Blum said.

Blum's car was parked in the parking lot of the kitchen compound, so he decided to check out the kitchen compound to see what was going on. Most of the activity was taking place in the horseman's lounge and as he walked by, he waved to a few people — Herb Paley was already seated, his shirt-sleeves rolled up — and shook his head to invitations that he join in the card playing. Blum then decided to have a quick cup of coffee in the kitchen — where he agreed to share his views on betting.

"I never bet," he said. "The public thinks that the jockey has an edge when it comes to betting. Trainers are the same. They'll say, 'Who do you think we have to beat?' Well, I would never say we have to beat the three horse. I always think it's best to say, 'We've got to beat them all.' Which you do.

"I'm such a lousy handicapper because I like almost anything I ride. Like today I ride five horses. Well, I like all of them. I know damned well I can't win five. Two or three of them can win. Maybe four. Highly improbable, but possible.

"So I figure for each race I have a chance because I know I'm letting that horse run. I know I'm going to get out of him the best that he's got in him, the best he's got to give. So looking at it like that, if I were a bettor, I would bet on every one of my horses. Thank heaven I'm not a bettor.

"But the public thinks that the jockey knows who's going to win. Sometimes he does. We have a feeling sometimes in the respect that . . . I might ride a horse today, for instance, that might get into trouble. He might get some traffic problems. He might get beat by two or three lengths, run a real good race, and if not for that problem he might have won. Okay. So I know that. A lot of people watching the race don't know that. So there I have an edge. The next time, if he runs in the same company, well, he should have a chance; provided the racetrack is the same, the conditions are the same, the same breaks come the same way, except for the fact that he doesn't get into trouble.

"Also, a lot of horses we ride in the afternoon we exercise in the morning, so here again you have an edge because the public has probably never seen that horse before. They don't know anything about the horse.

"At least you know if he's going sound, if he feels good, if he's strong under you. If he is, in the morning, he should run well in the afternoon. There we know more than the average fan. But for all we know, there's still much we don't know. Things can happen that we don't know are going to happen. Like the horse may feel well that morning, and in the afternoon he may feel lousy. Horses are like that. They may feel great in the morning, all on their toes and frisky and full of the devil, and in the afternoon they come to the paddock, they're dead. I don't know why. Maybe the crowd shakes them up.

"Still, the public thinks the jockey knows who's going to win, and because of this, they go around thinking that jockeys are rich guys. That's about as far from the truth as you can get. Jockeys are not rich. If they were they wouldn't be risking their lives day in and day out.

"Riding is a thrill for a few years, for the first few years, and it's nice work for the next few years, but after those fifteen to twenty years, it's work. You get up riding through rain, and mud, and cold weather, and a lot of times it's uncomfortable and you don't want to do it. But you do it because it's your job and you have to do it."

In his car, Walter Blum waved. He had to be back in a little over an hour and needed some rest.

This, the week of his 4,000, had been a week of great pressure for him, and it was not yet over. Months before he had talked enthusiastically about attaining 4,000, and it still meant much to him — after all, it was a sort of crowning — but complete satisfaction was lost to him when his father had died, a couple of weeks before, in Florida. Not being a demonstrative person, he nursed the grief in silence. (He would say, "We were very close.")

Upon his return from the funeral, there was concern as to how the loss would affect his performance. All fears were dispelled when he quickly reestablished himself by winning seven races in the first week of his return. There were those who said that never before had he ridden with such fury.

He was still riding with the same doggedness, determined, obviously, to prove to himself and to those who watched him closely that he was first and foremost a professional. There had been times before when he had been counted out and had come back stronger than before. Walter Blum had an abiding admiration for persons who triumphed over hardship. He counted himself among them. He took pride in his resiliency. Events, circumstances could bend him, but nothing short of death would break him.

When you go out there you have one foot in the hospital, the other foot in the cemetery. — Jacinto Vasquez

Chapter 21

Around noon, when most of the jockeys were already in the jockeys' room, Phil Sage, a mutuel clerk, wheeled himself in a wheelchair, past every locker. He smiled — it was a warm, kindly smile, paternal — and everybody, when his turn came, smiled back and said something like, "How's it going, Phil?" The jockeys who had been making the usual locker room noises piped down abruptly and grew solemn. The usual levity was suspended. Each man, in his own way, was paying tribute to Phil Sage, to Phil Sage and his gallantry and, at the same time, proffering a moment's meditative silence to the impartial gods of chance.

Phil Sage had been a rider for twenty-five years, good if not outstanding. His career spanned the years 1933 to 1958, and it ended where it started, at Charles Town. There, one morning in 1958, Phil Sage was exercising a horse, accompanied by another rider, Carl Gambardella. Astride their mounts, the two, lunging from the gate and picking up speed, were suddenly confronted by a riderless, spooked two-year-old, which had somehow gotten onto the track.

All three horses were killed, two on the spot. Gambardella was spared serious injury. Sage was paralyzed from the mid-section down, for life. He had to adjust to the life of a paraplegic.

Not only did he adjust, but with the help of the Jockey's Guild, of which he had been a founding member and over which Walter Blum now presided, he overcame his handicap in masterful style. The tragedy left him far from bitter. He was as genial and easy-going as ever.

For the rider there are no guarantees. There is nothing in his contract that specifies that he will not be killed or paralyzed. For all the risk, he is simply a man doing his job. He checks in at six or seven in the morning and checks out late in the afternoon; anywhere in between he might ride the precursor of death. When he dies his violent death, he is mourned by his family and the family of jocks, who add another name to the long list. A two-paragraph article in the sports page of the newspaper mentions his age and his two most famous races. The headline reads, "So and So, Winner of the 1955 Such and Such, Killed in Spill."

The jockey who survives a bad spill is also no hero to the people in the stands. He certainly cannot count on their sympathy. He can hope only for the understanding of his peers. For only a fellow rider understands what it means to go out there, afternoon or morning. This is the bond that holds jocks together. They have nothing else in common. They are not part of a team. Each man is out for himself. This is why the jockeys' room is so different from any other locker room. Togetherness, team spirit, is nonexistent, as well it has to be; in a sport that pits man against man, cooperation is tantamount to collusion.

Still, in the jockeys' room, they laugh together and joke together, often to hide and submerge the fear — and the presence of a man such as Phil Sage is always a reminder.

In the jocks' room a jock is seldom seen sitting or standing still. He is always moving, always talking, everything but thinking. The closer it gets to post, the less he wants to think. What else will it bring on but depression — and what Henry Block liked to call "that fear thing."

Some riders sit in front of their lockers and quake, their hands trembling so badly they cannot button up their silks. These are the younger ones, usually, or older ones who have just come off a bad spill.

The riders who sit in front of their lockers and quake later often are a hazard to themselves and anyone who draws close. They see a hole and from fear back off, hooking heels with the horse coming from behind. If it is not fear, it is loss of split-second timing, and when a rider loses his timing, he is worthless — or dangerous. A hole between horses lasts no more than an instant; it ebbs and flows. There is that fraction of a second that invites the rider to bully through, and if he has the alertness and courage he will, thinking nothing of brushing up against the horses on either side. Sometimes the gap between horses is so wide that it takes no courage to get in, but for some riders, the safety of the pack always is preferable. Along a straightaway the rider presented with a gap has to make a split-second decision, and when convinced, by that feel in his hands, that he has the horse — enough horse — he has to charge his way through with no regard for the consequences. When he stops to think, he is lost. He has to act and think all at once.

Then nce he decides to go, he has to decide whether to keep going or gra lly to back off because the horses on either side don't part like s inging doors. At times they stick together as though glued. Usually they part. When they do not, courage is called for from both horse and rider. At this point, coming between teamed horses at some forty miles an hour, the horse must use his powerful head to nudge and butt the hindquarters of his adversaries on either side, to force an opening made smooth and pliable by the sweat of his side-by-side rivals. Then, entry secure, he thrusts further, finally into daylight, and draws away nice and clean — to the immense satisfaction of his rider. For every rider, no moment in a race equals for sweet pleasure that of coming out of the darkness of a pack into the clearness of daylight.

If there are horses that are up to the challenge, there are riders who are not. These ponder and wonder about that hole. They see that that horse on the left has bad action, that he is swinging his right foreleg out, say, and they hesitate. And that hesitation, when it comes in a field closely bunched, likely results in a spill — riders flying over horses and horses flying over riders. (A horse will do his best to avoid stepping on a fallen rider. There was one instance, recently, in which in order to avoid stepping on his fallen rider, a horse made a somersault and caused his own death.)

So there are riders who ride with courage, and there are riders who ride with fear. Both are at the mercy of chance.

Along the backstretch, speaking of riders of courage, three names are most prominently mentioned: Henry Block, Donald Weipert, and Walter Blum. There are, of course, plenty of others. Frank Lovato, the rider who once had beaten Damascus and Eddie Arcaro, was once virtually carried off the field, into an ambulance, limb by limb. He returned. Then there was Jimmy Moseley, Carlos Barrera, Karl Korte, Paul Kallai, Mick Miceli, and many others.

Henry Block, in Blum's season of 4,000, had given up riding in favor of training when it appeared to him that he was coming down with heart trouble. He was having chest pains, which later were diagnosed as muscle spasms.

Henry Block had made a lot of money as a rider, much of it riding for Danny Perlsweig. Though he is somewhere in his upper thirties (when they get past thirty, jockeys get sensitive about their age), he is still very youthful, actually boyish, in temperament and outlook. He does not take himself too seriously and has a fine sense of humor. He is built wide and square and has a round face.

In 1954, at Garden State, Henry Block had a spill that nearly ended his career as a rider, as a trainer, and as a person.

"That day," he recalled one morning in front of his shed row, "I went immediately to the front, out of the gate, and I stayed in the front to the middle of the backside, and about the middle of the backside, this other rider and his horse came to me and we raced as a team to the half-mile pole.

"Now as he came to me, he kind of went by me by a head, and just pushed me in close enough to where I was pinned next to the fence. So I looked over to the other rider and I talked to him. I said, 'Fella, you know you're pushing me down to the fence. I'll never make the turn. Give me a chance to get the hell out of here.'

"He says, 'Okay! Okay!'

"So we went along another four or five strides. I says, 'Fella, when we go into that turn you're going to smother me now. You're making it tough for me.' He says, 'All right, all right; you're okay.'

"He kept holding his conversation with me but I wasn't getting anything out of the conversation.

"When we got to the turn, he had me outrun by a neck. He was slowly getting away from me. So if I hadn't held this conversation with him I would have backed the hell out of there. But now, as we got to the turn, I was so close to the fence that my horse couldn't change leads. So he just pushed me to the fence. I actually hit the fence the length of a car before I fell. My horse just smothered the fence."

As a result, Henry Block had a broken neck and a broken collar bone, requiring a plate and four screws. He also developed blood clots in the leg that had scraped the fence the length of a car. The plate and four screws remained in his body for the rest of his riding career.

"It took me months to recuperate, but I couldn't wait to get back. When I got back, I have to say, quite truthfully, I was a bit apprehensive. The only time in my life.

"I rode a horse, that first time back, in the number one post position, and naturally I went into the gate first. And when they closed that door I said to myself, 'Jeez, you know, here I am, that bell's going to ring in a minute, and that door's going to open, I wonder if I'm going to fall on my head again?'

"The longer I was in there the longer I kept scratching my ass. 'Jesus, I wish the hell it would open up.' Shit or get off the pot, so to speak.

"But that horse run and he won and I didn't have that feeling no more."

That spill at Garden had had its light moment (in retrospect). "You talk about something funny. We're laying on the ground, this other boy and me; when I fell this other boy fell with me.

So I'm laying on the ground, I'm seeing stars and stripes out of my eyes, and this other boy runs over to me and he says, 'Henry, Henry, you all right?' I said, 'Lay down, you asshole. If you don't lay down the ambulance isn't going to come and get us.' "

Henry Block laughed.

"So he laid down. Muddier 'an hell. It was muddier 'an hell."

Henry Block was presently conditioning four horses. Of those four, only two were qualified to run. One, having fractured a knee in a recent race, would have to be destroyed. Another was laid up with various injuries. Henry Block was seriously thinking of becoming a jockey again. At the moment, however, he had a broken toe. Earlier in the day, a cowboy trainer had challenged Henry Block to a footrace.

"You don't smoke, right?" the cowboy trainer had said.

"Right."

"You don't drink, right?"

"Right."

"You keep pretty fit, right?"

"Yeah."

"Well, I smoke two packs a day. I drink like a sieve. I fuck around with women all night. I'm forty-eight. About ten years older 'an you. And I'll bet you a hundred dollars I can outrun you. Right now. Two hundred dollars. Right now."

"I got a broken toe."

"Sure."

In time, Henry Block would go back to riding. He would, he knew, be pushing his luck.

"You never know the kind of horse you're going to get on. You can get on a real screwball and he can hurt anybody, including himself. But you can't let that fear thing get to you. Besides, experience tells you how to protect yourself.

"Horses tip you off if they're going to do something. A nervous horse, his heart beats a mile a minute. And a mean horse, well, chances are he's been mean before you got him. And he'll tip you off he's mean.

"A mean horse won't hurt you because you're ready for him. A scared horse will hurt you because at any given time he can flip his lid and he can getcha. A mean horse, you don't give him no shot to hurt you. You get the one you're confident about, and you're petting him, and all of a sudden his foot's in your mouth."

That, Henry Block said, was not a good feeling.

"A rider," he said, "is the most overpaid guy when he's just riding. But when he falls and gets hurt, he's never paid enough."

Donald Weipert came from a proud Philadelphia racing family. There was the father, Gerard, and his four sons. Two of the sons became trainers; the other two, riders. Bobby Weipert rode for about a year and quit when he found himself getting up mornings weak and dizzy from the fasting. That left Donald.

On March 11, 1972, at Hialeah, Donald Weipert, aged twenty, brought to the post for the first race of the afternoon a horse called Laff A Lot. At this point Donald Weipert, a three-bug apprentice, was well up in the standings, contesting Walter Blum for leading rider honors. The horse, Laff A Lot, was easy handling in the gate, and the break was nice and even. As the field approached the half-mile pole, one horse kept lugging in on Donald Weipert. He shouted at its rider to straighten up. But the errant horse, now right alongside Laff A Lot, continued lugging in. "You're crowding me," Donald Weipert yelled out. But the horse kept lugging in and, finally, hooked hooves with Laff A Lot, causing him to lose his balance and fall, in a quick, sudden moment, to his knees. Donald Weipert was tossed in the air and landed some thirty feet away in a dive, front first.

The impact scraped all the skin off Donald Weipert's face, from chin to forehead. But that was the least of his injuries. Later, at North Shore Hospital, it was discovered that he had a broken back, having crushed the eighth and ninth vertebrae. The doctors were not concerned with Donald Weipert's being able to ride again. They were concerned with his being able to walk again. The chances were that he wouldn't.

Donald Weipert spent thirteen days in the intensive care unit of North Shore Hospital. At the age of twenty he had the prospect of spending the rest of his life in a wheelchair. In the intensive care unit he showed no signs of progress in the first few days. He had given up.

A year later he was riding again.

"Most of the credit has to go to Walter Blum," he said. "The fourth or fifth day I was in intensive care, when I was at my worst, Walter Blum visited me. Nobody was allowed in except my immediate family but Blum got in by telling the nurses that he was my brother or something. He talked to me for a long time. He told me I couldn't give up. He told me the same thing had happened to him and he didn't give up. He said if I put my mind to it and didn't give up I would be okay. He kept talking to me like that and after he left, I don't know, I started getting better. I can't really say I got better because of Blum's visit. But I can say that because of him my morale shot way up, and I started believing in myself again."

Chapter 22

Nineteen sixty-four was fated to be a year of ambiguity for Walter Blum. For the better part of it — in fact, up to the last day of it — he was a rider to be envied. Indeed, at a time when both the Latins and the Americans were at their best, he was the standout. He started the year as the focus of attention by virtue of having completed 1963 with 360 wins and the riding championship. The newspapers hailed him the nation's "Racing King." As 1964 progressed it was obvious he would be racing king again. By the summer of 1964, he was, in terms of wins, far ahead of the pack, pulling away from the Shoemakers, the Arcaros, the Baezas, the Ycazas, in the same style that marked him as a rider: quick start, strong finish. But he was not to be judged on quantity alone. Two of his most notable successes came aboard Gun Bow, against the regal Kelso, the one thoroughbred whose claim to greatness would never be questioned.

The Kelso-Gun Bow duels were gems. In the first interesting match-up of the two, July 25, 1964, in the Brooklyn Handicap, Kelso, usually the picture of serenity in the starting gate, acted up under his rider, Ismael Valenzuela, and got off to a stumbled start, never to challenge Gun Bow for the lead. Gun Bow won going away.

However, the victory, because of the start, was not convincing. Nonetheless, when Gun Bow and Kelso met up again a few weeks later in the mile and an eighth Aqueduct Stakes, Gun Bow went off the favorite. Walter Blum got him off to a clear advantage and began eating up distance. Then, when it appeared he had the track to himself, Ismael Valenzuela roused his mount to contention, and Kelso and Gun Bow hooked up in a duel that had the spectators in ecstasy. Kelso kept coming to Gun Bow, kept passing Gun Bow, but he could not dispose of him. The seven-year-old Gun Bow simply refused to give in to a four-year-old upstart. They went to the wire neck and neck. Kelso was the victor, by three quarters of a length, but Gun Bow had served notice that he intended to work the same side of the street as Kelso.

A month later the two met again, in the Woodward Stakes, and the drama was heightened by the prospect of revenge. Walter Blum remembered this Woodward as his most thrilling race, recalling that it was the only time he actually heard the spectators in the stands. Ordinarily, he said, when you rode a race, you were oblivious to the crowd. But that day you could hear the crowd. Everybody was caught up in the spectacle and "you could feel the grandstand shaking."

This time Gun Bow did not go off on the lead alone. For this mile and a quarter event, Kelso matched the front-running Gun Bow stride for stride from the moment the gates were flung open. The two runners went head to head the entire distance. They swapped leads every other stride. Coming to the wire they were as one. At the wire there was no distinguishing between them. Finally, after a period of ascending suspense, the photo revealed that Kelso had crossed the finish line first by, in the words of the rider who came in second, "the slightest nose you ever saw."

Gun Bow never beat Kelso again and later he retired with earnings of $798,722; Kelso, in his lifetime, won the still unequaled sum of $1,977,896. Gun Bow went down as Walter Blum's all-time favorite mount. To be sure, Blum always remembered with fondness the likes of Pass Catcher, on whom he upset

Canonero II in the 1971 Belmont, and Affectionately, and Reason To Hail, and Lady Pitt, and Summer Scandal, and Venomous; but only Gun Bow beat the reigning king of thoroughbreds — twice.

So 1964 had its wonderful moments, and in December of that year, the riding title firm in his grasp on the strength of 324 victories, Blum set out for California to vacation and prepare himself for the upcoming Santa Anita meeting.

In California, he spent a restful week, enjoying the blue skies, the sun, and the water. These few days away from the track were days to be savored. In the past ten years no day had gone by when he had not been on a horse. The past two years had been especially hard. He had won a total of 684 races. He had lost over four times that many. Combined, they made for a very tired rider.

As Christmas and the Santa Anita meeting drew near, he began paying leisurely visits to the Santa Anita backside, limbering up horses and getting himself ready for a meeting he was determined to finish as leading rider. Slowly he worked himself into shape.

Santa Anita seemed a fine place for Walter Blum to close out his year. There was the sun, the warm weather, and the California horseplayers, who knew him well. He had raced here many times before, winning plenty of times before. So when the meeting opened in late December, he was greeted with warm applause.

In this congenial setting Walter Blum rode winners and losers for the next few days. On the last day of the year, on the day his championship title stood as official, Walter Blum mounted a horse called Country Squire for a six-furlong race.

Walter Blum had ridden Country Squire before and had enjoyed riding him. He was an easy horse to ride. This time he was as easy as ever. He warmed up nicely in the moments leading to post and was relaxed. He got into the gate smoothly and got out of the gate smoothly. He took the early lead and maintained it to the far turn, approaching it in mounting speed. Rounding the far turn, setting himself up for the dash to the wire, he was in full run. Coming to the quarter pole he was ahead of the field by some three lengths. But in coming to the quarter pole, he shifted his weight for the turn from his right to his left, and his left foreleg snapped and broke. The break halted him in midstride. He hobbled forward a stride or two, tried to put pressure on the disabled foreleg, testing it. Then he drew the foreleg back into himself and sank to the ground. Walter Blum tried to hold him up on his feet but couldn't. Horse and rider went down.

Walter Blum rolled himself up into a ball and prayed that the field was safely by him. It was — except for one straggler, which booted Walter Blum from the quarter pole to the one-eighth pole.

When he regained consciousness in the hospital the next day he was certain he was "split in half," so great was the pain. The diagnosis was contusions, abrasions, three broken ribs, and extensive damage to the fourth, fifth, and sixth lumbar vertebrae — in short, a broken back.

The newspapers paid due attention to the fallen racing hero. One newspaper carried the banner: "Racing King Near Death." Another ran this headline: "Death in the Afternoon." He was all but buried.

In the days that followed Walter Blum read these accounts of his imminent demise. He was not cheered.

With the exception of one, the doctors that attended him were likewise no source of consolation. The most optimistic of them said recovery, if it came, would not come before a year. The most pessimistic of them — the majority — assured him that he would never regain the use of his legs.

He was, indeed, broken in half.

The exception was Dr. Robert K. Kerlan, the team physician of the Los Angeles Lakers. He promised his patient a speedy and complete restoration, telling him to pay no mind to the pessimists and to quit believing what the newspapers were saying.

At first Blum did not know what to make of Kerlan. Was Kerlan putting him on? Giving him false hope? The newspapers, after all, and the other doctors, were most persuasive and only a fool would unequivocally ignore their prophecies.

But Kerlan was steadfast, and from Kerlan Blum drew strength of spirit.

Walter Blum, in brace and all, was out of the hospital some thirty days after he was brought in, walking out on his own two legs — to the amazement of doctors and nurses. But the job of recovery had just begun.

Kerlan put Blum under an intensive therapy program, which included warm compresses to the back and the lifting of leg weights to fortify the weakened muscles. Each morning, Harold Wiscman, Blum's agent, picked him up at his home in Arcadia and drove him to Kerlan's office in Los Angeles.

After three weeks of this regimen Walter Blum was convinced he would be fine. He was regaining his strength, physically and mentally. Now it was only a question of how soon he would be back, and he was in a hurry to get back. He wanted to finish what he had started, the Santa Anita meeting. He had something to prove, though he was not sure what it was he had to prove. Perhaps, he later admitted, it was a matter of ego.

In any case, he returned to Santa Anita in late February 1965, not two months since he had been scraped off the field. He approached his first mount of the day with caution. He felt weak in the legs and the back. He had not had the feel of a horse under him for some two months and was overcome with the novelty of it. He was truly nervous and excited and had no winners that day.

The following day he won a race and in the winner's circle accepted with grace the crowd's genuine display of gratitude. In the next two — final — weeks of the Santa Anita meeting he went on to win a remarkable total of twelve races.

After that, in the spring that followed, he finished the Garden State meeting as leading rider.

A jockey just has to be lucky to go through his career of riding and not get seriously injured, at one time or another.

Willie Shoemaker, for instance, has been riding about twenty-two years now, and in twenty years he never had an accident. He went the whole twenty years without having an accident — a serious accident. I don't think he broke a bone in his body, riding.

And all at once he fell and broke his femur. He had quite a tough time with that and, in fact, he was out a year. Then he came back and started riding again, and he rode about two more months and damned if a horse didn't turn over backwards with him at Hollywood Park and crack his spleen or something.

But he healed and came out pretty well, and now he's been riding ever since without any problem.

But a jockey never really knows about injuries. They can just happen.

There are jockeys no sooner do they get up than they get hurt again. They're just accident prone, I guess. They're the unlucky ones, I guess. And the other ones are just lucky. I know of cases where jockeys have had falls through the years and as they ride and get a little older they become more and more leery, about, say, going into certain holes. They'll hesitate about going into a hole that five years ago they would have gone into without even thinking about it. When a jockey starts doing that he starts riding bad and he starts on his way out.

Jockeys themselves know quicker than anybody when they start getting that way. It's similar to a bullfighter that gets gored once or twice and doesn't want to face the bull again. A lot of riders, a few of them rather, when they realize that the fear is there, they start to ease away from riding and they look for other things. Because it's not really good for a jockey to ride if he's scared, or if he's even worried about getting hurt or having an accident. That slight hesitation when he comes to a hole, why that can cost him a race, a life, anything.

But I don't think a rider gets that way after just one spill. I think it's a thing that happens after a series of different spills.

Thank God it hasn't happened to me yet. I find myself, when I ride, I'll see a situation arise that I should take advantage of, I'll take advantage of it without thinking about getting hurt. I know I can get hurt, but I don't go into that hole thinking about getting hurt. I just make sure I've got enough room to go there and should be going there at that time. If I do go up in there and do get stopped or do get shut off or even fall, it's something that just happened. It just had to happen. It could have been that I went up in there without enough room, or in not enough time.

Sometimes, however, when you do make a move like that and you do get up in there and it might have been the right move to make, you still can get shut off after you get in there, and get dropped. So it's a risky business, riding, as we all know.

But you take that into consideration when you start — and

actually just living is a risky business. Driving a car is risky too.

Some people wonder which part of the racetrack is most dangerous. I can't really say. You can get hurt anywhere. You can get hurt warming up a horse before the race, and a lot of riders do get hurt that way. The horse becomes fractious when he sees the crowd, or when he sees a piece of paper come flying by, or some clown waves his hands in his face on his way to the post. Because of these clowns I don't like to keep my horse too close to the fans Sometimes they'll yell out, "Oh, there's my horse," and get him scared.

So all in all you can get hurt anywhere on the racetrack. Walking to the post. In the gate.

In the gate is a very dangerous spot. I guess I would have to say that's the most dangerous spot. Because you're caged in with an animal. A thousand pound animal. If he gets wild in there, you're at his mercy.

They can just crush you in there. They can fall over backwards, which they very often do, and when they do — with those backup steel doors closed behind you, you falling on top of those doors, with the horse on top of you, pal, you've had it. You're going to be in a wheelchair like Phil Sage.

But when you feel a horse go up in the air like that, you get ready to get the hell off him, and finally when he does get so high, on his way over, you should be off him by then. Your reflexes should have you off him, and ninety-nine times out of a hundred you do get off him. But there are times when a horse will do it so quickly you can't get off him. Or you'll try to get off him and get your foot hung up and your foot might get caught in there, and you break a leg.

Leaving the gate, if your horse stumbles, you can, like I did one day recently, fall off as well.

I've ridden this horse, Prince of Truth, any number of times I've won on him quite a few times. He's really a nice horse to ride. He's quick. Soon as the gate opens, he's gone. So this one day he was in the gate and was like he should have been, on his feet, looking down the racetrack. Then I don't know what happened to him, whether he stumbled or tripped himself or overstepped or what. When the gate flew open he jumped out of there and when he did, he stumbled and he stumbled far enough to pull me over his head. I tried to get him back on his feet, but he was down. He was just down. Almost completely down. And I just got flung over his head, and I was lucky I didn't get hurt.

But back to the gate itself, the worst thing that can happen to you in the gate is that your horse flips. You don't want to be on a horse that flips. That can cut you right in half. I would say if a horse lands on you like that, you'll never walk again.

I have, though, ridden horses that flipped with me once, and I've ridden them back again. You do that because you know the horse has got some ability and he can win. That's the name of the whole game, is to try and win a race.

Recently I've been riding a horse called Mrs. Lot. Mrs. Lot is about a $5,000 horse. That's what she's actually worth. Sometimes she runs for $6,500, $7,500. Now she flipped with me once. She flipped with another jockey once. This other jockey rode her one day, and I just happened to notice her. I never saw her before in my life, but I noticed her in the post parade. She was crazy. But the rider was fighting her. He was trying to manhandle her. When she got in the gate, she flipped, and I said, "Man, what the hell is her name? I don't want to ride that son of a bitch."

So when the race was over I forgot about Mrs. Lot. Two weeks later she was in, and I was named on her.

And I said to myself, "Oh, I remember that horse. She's a little nuts."

But you can't tell the man, "Look, I'm scared of that horse. I don't want to ride her."

So you go out there and you ride the horse and you try to outsmart her. So I got on her and she was a little fractious, and I petted her and bullshitted her — "Oh, honey, oh, sweetheart" — and right away, man, she calmed down great.

I got her to the post exceptionally well. I didn't fight her too much, and she got over there really well. So she's in the gate and I said to the assistant starter, "You know this horse?" He said, "Yeah, I know her. Do you know her?" I said, "Yeah, I know her." He said, "Well, you just sit still on her." I said, "Okay. I'm going to relax on her. But just you relax with her."

He held her in the gate, calmed her down, held her head straight. I wanted her to think I wasn't even on her. And in the gate she didn't know I was there. I mean I just froze on her. The only way I was going to move on her was if she went to flip.

Well, that's the way she walked in the gate, and I gave her her head, I turned loose of her reins, grabbed a handful of mane, and I stood there like that, and the guy held her straight, without forcing her — he just bullshitted her and talked to her — and maintained her head until the break came. When the break came, man, she was gone. She was on the lead and she won.

She won real easy, too, that day. So I thought, what a wonderful job I did! What a great rider I am!

I didn't say anything to my agent about riding her back. I figured if he wants to ride her back I'll ride her.

Well, I rode her back. And I got her into the gate again real good, and when we were in the gate, man, she flipped. She flipped so fast I didn't know which way she went. I didn't know which way I went. She flipped, and she threw me off.

I didn't jump off. Man, she just went up in the air and I was off her. Lucky I landed clear of her because she came right down on those doors.

They got her back on her feet, and the vet didn't scratch her. He wanted me to get back on her. And I didn't no more want to climb back on her than I wanted to get punched in the mouth. I mean she scared me because I knew I couldn't do nothing with her.

But I did climb back on her, and I did ride her. They tailed her. She didn't break good that day because I think horses that are tailed never break good anyway. I don't like to have them tailed, if they don't have to be. But anyway, she didn't break good that day. She didn't run good either. I told my agent that's it — I don't want to ride her no more.

So horses like that will frighten you. Horses like that you don't want to ride. But again, you come off a race like that, where you got spilled, and in the next race you go back in the gate not even thinking about what happened. Not even thinking about it happening. Until, of course, it happens.

Now, when it happens, if you don't get scared, you're a damned jerk. There's something wrong with you. But you come back.

I remember years and years ago I used to ride a horse called Elberwhirl. He was an old horse, been racing for years, and he wasn't particularly rough during the race, during the actual running he could run a little bit.

But he was really rough in the paddock. He was exceptionally rough walking out to the track. And he was a kook on the track, walking to the post, warming up and everything. And in the gate, he was just a bad horse. He was a bad actor. Eventually they ruled him off. He was just a damned nut.

But he could run some and he was sound and the stewards didn't rule him off until late in his life.

So this guy from Maryland had him, and I used to ride for him, this trainer. I rode other horses for the guy and when it came to ride this one I couldn't tell him I was afraid. But I was afraid to ride the horse, and I got on him one day at Monmouth, and he pulled a real show out there in the paddock. He lunged over fences and he cleared the whole damned paddock area that one day — and I was on him. The only reason I didn't get off him was because he wouldn't stand still long enough for me to get off him. I couldn't get off the son of a bitch.

Sometimes you get on a horse and he's doing so much with you, for one reason or another you can't unglue yourself from the son of a bitch.

And this was one of those times. I couldn't get off this horse. He was just all over the place, lunging up in the trees, on top of the groom.

Finally, when he couldn't get me off, he reached around with his mouth and he grabbed ahold of my pants, and he just tore my pants off my ass. Just tore them right off. So we continued on out to the track and I rode the horse with half my ass hanging out.

But it doesn't always end that funny. It didn't for Phil Sage — and what can you say about a guy like Phil Sage. He's just the greatest, the way he came back and everything. He never asked for pity, nothing. Everybody respects him for what he's done with his life. He's not going to be a rich guy anymore but he works every day, and he's got a wonderful wife who helps him along. And he does everything he can to make a buck. He doesn't let his handicap overcome his life. He knows he has to live that way, and he makes the best of it. I think that's great. All the guys respect him for the way he handles himself. He never complains. Never.

There's another boy that just got spilled and is now a paraplegic — and he can't cut it. He's going crazy. Poor kid's going crazy. He doesn't know what to do. He's a real nice kid. Mentally, man, he went to pieces. He was always a fun guy, loved life, and he lived it to the fullest. He'll never walk again.

We've done all we can. The Jockey's Guild.

We rehabilitate them, we take care of all the bills, and eventually place them in various jobs. Some of them do very well in their handicapped state. Like Phil Sage. We have another kid who became a paraplegic, went back to school, and became a lawyer. He's now a fine lawyer, making a hell of a living.

But it's something that these kids have to readjust themselves to. They have to rehabilitate themselves. They have to be willing. The most the Jockey's Guild can do is give these kids their confidence back and show them that they can survive life.

For some of them it works, for some of them it doesn't. Some of them go to pieces.

I can imagine how you would just go to pieces. I think I would.

Now I could handle a spill like I had in 1964. But I don't know if I could handle being a paraplegic. I don't know if I could cut it, man. I've always felt that way, and I've always felt that way about being blind.

For years I guarded it as a secret, that I was completely blind in my right eye. I didn't want people to know it because I thought they would stop me from riding. I thought they wouldn't put me on horses.

People found out that I was blind in my right eye only the past few years.

They found out about it first in New York. In New York, the first of every year when you ride there, they give you a pretty rigid physical. They test you from your asshole to your elbow. So just a few years ago they line me up to read the chart, and the nurse said, "Cover your left eye." Now this nurse had been taking my physical for years, and when I told her I was blind in my right eye, she said, "Oh, my God. When did that happen?" So I told her it's been that way all my life. The only reason you never realized it before was because I used to switch hands instead of eyes.

Anyway, when people realized that I could ride with one eye, no problem. So now it doesn't bother me.

The point is, I always thought, even when I was a kid, what would I do if I lost my sight in my left eye? And that thought always plagues my mind. Because I couldn't cut it if I was blind. I don't think I could.

Maybe I could. Maybe if the reality finally came, or if it should happen, or does — God forbid — maybe I could cut it.

But I really don't think I could make it. I would want to be dead or something.

Maybe that's the way those guys feel when they got those accidents. They feel that their whole world is crumbled down and they're no longer useful to themselves or anybody else, and they get really uptight, and I can understand that.

Thursday Afternoon

Chapter 23

At precisely 1:40, that is, twenty minutes to the start of the first race of the afternoon, Sam Boulmetis was threading his way through the crowd in the grandstand on his way to the elevator that would take him up to the roof. He walked quickly and bounced as he walked. He was dressed conservatively, in a dark suit, and wore a bow tie. A few horseplayers recognized him and said, "There's Sam Boulmetis. Remember him?"

Sam Boulmetis was a jockey whose good years did not end with retirement. After he retired, he was installed in racing's Hall of Fame and later became a steward, which, next to being a member of the Racing Commission, was as high as you could go.

As a jockey he had lived by the decisions of others; as a steward he made the decisions others lived by. The decisions he made were as binding and inflictive as any judge's. Earlier in the day he and the two other stewards, Keene Daingerfield and Richard Lawrenson, had sat in judgment over a series of cases that would have tested a Solomon.

In one instance a trainer whose horses were stabled in his father's shed row wanted to move onto a shed row of his own. The matter was one of accountability. His horses were being mistaken for his father's. Only last week he and his father had horses entered in the same race and the racing secretary came close to marking them as a joint entry. Perhaps separate quarters would end the confusion. After conferring with his partners, Sam Boulmetis ruled that because there was a shortage of vacant shed rows the young trainer would have to remain under his father's roof, for the time being. As for entering a race his father had already entered, Sam Boulmetis' suggestion was: Don't.

In another instance, a rider originally from Greece requested permission to exercise and ride horses at Monmouth. In California a few days before he had been barred from racing for failure to renew his visa. "The stewards told me I can race again when I am okay with immigration," he said. He said he was now okay with immigration and presented the papers to prove it. After Sam Boulmetis read the papers, he said, "Fine with me. The trouble is, only the state that ruled you off can install you again. Right now you're in bad standing with California. What I'm going to do is call up the stewards in California later on and get them to give me the okay. I can't call them right now because of the time difference. Once I get the okay you can go right to work." The youth from Greece said he did not have a penny in his pocket and needed to go to work this minute. "Do you have a trainer?" Sam Boulmetis asked. "Yes," said the youth from Greece, mentioning a name. "Well, you tell him he'll probably be able to put you to work tomorrow morning and in the meantime to give you a few dollars. You tell him Sam Boulmetis said to give you a few dollars. Okay?" The youth smiled and said, "Thank you very much. You are very kind."

Exercising this kind of authority was pleasing to Sam Boulmetis, and the pleasure was evident in the way he carried himself. The stance was intractably erect, especially in the company of subordinates, the eyes clear and forward-looking, the head defiantly upright. A mane of brown-silver added to the quality of eminence.

Sam Boulmetis had been one of the smart ones. He had sidestepped the trap that lured aging athletes into believing that that comeback year was one year away and in the end made mental cases of boxers and cripples and boozers of jockeys. For Sam Boulmetis there had been no boozing or self-pity with the realization that the riding years were over.

And the riding years were over when the timing was gone. In other sports, it was the legs that went first. In riding it was the timing.

So when Sam Boulmetis quit, he quit with his reflexes dulled but his reputation intact — enhanced, in fact, for having the presence of mind to know when enough was enough. Knowing that, he made a place for himself in his profession's hierarchy.

When the elevator came for him, he stepped in and ascended to the top floor. There he took the long, narrow, airless passage that led to the stewards' room. The stewards, the placing judges, and the press all shared the same lounge. When Sam Boulmetis came in, a few newsmen watching a television screen nodded, and one of them mentioned the weather, how nice it was. Sam Boulmetis agreed the weather was nice. He then proceeded briskly to the stewards' room, where Richard Lawrenson and Keene Daingerfield were already setting up. Richard Lawrenson was built thin and lanky, and his chin jutted out. Of the three stewards he was the most pleasant. Keene Daingerfield was the most distinguished. He had the authoritative air of a high school principal: never smiled, always frowned. Under his suit jacket he wore a vest. His magisterial look was used most effectively in the disciplining of delinquent horsemen. Some rocked on their heels to his uncompromising glare. Keene Daingerfield was the steward who represented the New Jersey Racing Commission. Richard Lawrenson and Sam Boulmetis were the appointees of the Monmouth Park Racing Association, serving under the approval of the Racing Commission.

Keene Daingerfield flicked the switches that regulated the in-house television. One switch panned the field. Another switch gave a head-on, close-up view of a race. A third switch ran the race backward. When the propriety of a race was in doubt, the questionable span was isolated, run backward and forward. Satisfied that the television was working properly, Keene

Daingerfield relaxed with a newspaper.

Sam Boulmetis stepped out onto the balcony. The balcony offered an unobstructed, panoramic view of the entire oval, the infield, and parts of the clubhouse and grandstand. He checked out the headsets that rested on a ledge. The headsets were connected to the microphones of the patrol judges, who were stationed on various points along the infield, high off the ground, in observation booths. As the field of horses approached and passed each patrol judge, he reported his impression. Beside each headset was a set of binoculars. During the running of a race two stewards observed it from the balcony, headsets and binoculars in place, and one steward remained indoors and watched it on the television. They took turns.

After checking out the equipment, Sam Boulmetis remained on the balcony to enjoy the warmth and make an accounting of the spectators down below. The fine weather had brought out a large crowd. Sam Boulmetis recognized a few faces, far up as he was. Most he didn't. On the clubhouse side, to his right, he recognized a jockey of days gone by, dressed grubbily. He waved down but could not draw his attention. Sam Boulmetis chuckled and shook his head. He then stretched and yawned and went back inside.

Below, in the rear, in the paddock, the horses for the first race of the afternoon were being saddled up amid an eager, happy group of onlookers, most of them — from the clubhouse side — tanned and radiant. While the horses were being saddled up, Sam Amico, the horse identifier, moved from stall to stall plying his trade. In his left hand he balanced a clipboard on which was a list of every horse in the race. With his free hand he grabbed the upper lip of each horse, turned the upper lip inside out, and took note of the tattoo marking, composed of letters and numbers. Horses have been identified this way since 1946 (at least in Thoroughbred Racing Association-member tracks). Before 1946, thoroughbreds were branded on the hoof or hide for the purpose of identification. This was not a very effective method, proving both painful and inaccurate. Very often, before 1946, thoroughbreds were not branded at all. This led to falsification of foal certificates and substitution. So you had ringers. There still are ringers, but, according to the Thoroughbred Racing Protective Bureau, there has not been a ringer case in a TRPB-supervised track in over twenty-five years. This is all due to the lip tattoo method of branding.

When the horse's tattoo marking in his upper lip matched his tattoo marking on Sam Amico's clipboard, he placed a check mark next to the horse's name and went on to another horse, just as reluctant: nobody, not even a horse, likes the idea of some jerk grabbing his lip and bending it in two.

When the markings do not match, trouble. The horse will be withdrawn and the trainer suspended, pending, as they say, an investigation. The investigation will be directed from TRPB headquarters in New York, where on file is a photograph of every tattoo of every horse ever branded. "We know," says a recent TRPB annual report, "where the horse was tattooed, on what date, the name of the technician who did the branding, the original Jockey Club certificate number and we can produce a picture of what the tattoo brand looks like."

There was, however, no question about the horses being run in the first race of this afternoon — for that matter, of any horse of any race during the meeting — and after Sam Amico finished his identifying, the horses, now saddled up and ready, some with blinkers, some without, some with shadow rolls, were led from the paddock to the walking ring, which they circled, prancingly, led by the shank by their grooms, while the owners and trainers exchanged pleasantries under the trees that shaded the walking ring.

At 1:46 the jockeys, in their neat, multicolored, incandescent silks, boots glistening in the sun, whip at the side, entered the walking ring, proudly — bullfighters disdainful of the crowd. They walked from the sun to the shade of the trees to their awaiting trainers and owners, and, after an introduction, if it was a first union of jockey and owner, or a fleeting polite inquiry as to health and well-being, discussed strategy.

At 1:47 the jockeys were boosted up on their horses. They did not, ever, climb up on their mounts via the stirrup iron — as one mounted most other horses — because thoroughbreds being the nervous, high-strung animals that they are react violently to so sudden a stress.

Up on their horses the jockeys touch-felt the saddle, the surcingle, and the girth — they did not want the saddle slipping off on them, as it occasionally did, costing a race at the least and a life at the most. Once on a horse called Princess Doubleday Walter Blum had a saddle slip on him and, consequently, could not, during the course of the race, get a solid grip of the reins. His instructions were to keep the filly off the pace in the early going. Her problem was that she had speed but could not rate herself and so used herself up. As it turned out, she got out in front and could not be restrained. Every time Blum tried to grab hold of the reins to subdue her, he slid back on the loose, carelessly applied saddle. Were it not for that, he would perhaps have beaten that year's champion filly, La Prevoyante. As it was, after leading the field and La Prevoyante, for the better part of the race, he was out of it where and when it counted most: the homestretch.

So the first thing a jockey did when he mounted his horse was examine the equipment. Then he fitted his feet into the irons.

At 1:49 the horses and their riders answered the call of the bugle and marched in numerical procession from the walking ring to the tunnel. The tunnel separated the clubhouse from the grandstand. On both sides, a crowd of spectators spread out along the rails. The tunnel was narrow, and the horses were close enough to the sides to be touched. They made formidable figures. On the clubhouse side of the tunnel a closed-circuit television hung overhead, and it was around this television that the agents gathered and watched the race and that the jockeys, coming back from a race, observed the rerun, leaning against the rail, dusty and sweaty, the losers looking to see what they had done wrong, the winner looking to see what he had done right. Sometimes, among the agents, angry words were exchanged during the watching of a rerun, when, for example, one agent thought that his boy had been bothered by another's.

Coming through the tunnel one by one onto the main track, in view of the spectators in the stands, the horses and their riders were bright and magnificent under the sun in their flashy colors. The procession, still in numerical order, marched left about thirty yards, then, making an about-turn, formed a half circle, and straightened out, heading right, in single file, except for the horses that were fractious. Then the procession broke up, as one horse after another cut the imaginary tie that linked him to the chain.

Now the riders were high off their seats mid-galloping their mounts to the starting gate. They would be seven minutes getting to the starting gate. In those seven minutes the horses would be warmed up.

As the horses went their individual ways past the clubhouse stands, the starter, Edward Blind, was already at the starting gate with his eight assistants. Edward Blind drew the program from his hip pocket and scanned the list of the nine horses that were coming his way. Of those nine horses two would need special attention. Edward Blind knew this from the notes in his program. The notes, which he had scribbled earlier in the morning, indicated that the number one horse, Ravenous, Walter Blum up, was particular in the gate and that the number three horse, Llantor, James Brophy up, was a first-time starter. Edward Blind, like all starters, made it a habit to go over the entire program each morning. He invariably came across horses he knew from before, and if any of these horses brought to mind an eccentricity, he made a note of it in his program in the space beside the horse's name. This way there were no surprises, for him or his assistants, and he knew which horse would be malleable, which would require two assistants, and which would have to be tailed, or brought in last.

Edward Blind had already decided that the two potentially troublesome runners, Ravenous and Llantor, would be brought in last. He now pointed this out to the assistants gathered around him. To the two assistants who would be responsible for Ravenous and Llantor, he offered words of caution.

With three minutes to post the horses — all two-year-olds, maidens — came postward. They were tight and tense and high off their feet. To each horse the starting gate represented final proof that he was about to be in a race, about to be tested among his peers. The first realization of the fact had come the day before when he was deprived of his feed; the second when in the morning he was fitted with a bridle instead of his usual halter; the third when he was uprooted from the back side to the front side, the center of attention of thousands of screaming humans; the fourth and most convincing and often the most fearsome proof was the sighting of the starting gate.

As the horses — some of them accompanied by ponies — came postward, the assistant starters went out to meet them, and Edward Blind, noting the three-minute deadline, quickly mounted the fifty or so steps to his observation booth in the infield, from where he would supervise and, through a microphone, mete out instructions.

With two minutes to go the horses circled the starting gate. Some of them were perspiring from the fear, kicking high off their hind legs, resisting the assistant starters. The assistant starters held on firmly to the bottom, lagging portion of the reins, while the jockeys held on and maneuvered with the portion of the reins in their grasp. As each assistant starter brought his assigned mount under control, he directed him into the starting stall, clamped the back doors shut (each starting stall had its own back door), then boosted himself onto the two slim planks on either side, remaining in this insecure position, over the horse, behind the rider, until the bell, when the horses were released.

The horses were all in now except for the one, Ravenous, the three, Llantor, and the four, Southern Legend, Paul Kallai up.

Southern Legend would approach his starting stall and just as soon, retreat. Edward Blind ordered that the horse be taken around again. Coming back to his stall the horse reared. Coming down he missed trampling the assistant starter by about a foot as his rider, Paul Kallai, went high in the air, landed hard on the saddle, and bounced up and down in it a few times until the horse settled.

When the horse was settled, the assistant starter said, "Now you be easy now. Ain't nobody gonna hurt ya."

Paul Kallai said, "Now you be good. Now you be good."

From his observation post Edward Blind instructed: "Get to him from the side, Jim."

The assistant starter moved out of the horse's line of vision and then snuck up on him from the left — thoroughbreds are always approached, and trained, from the left — quickly took hold of his reins and moved him into his cubicle, where he was still rank, threatening to flip.

"Tail him," Edward Blind said.

The horse's tail was placed over the top of the backup door. This way if he went up, he could not fall back, too far.

"Let's get going with the three," Edward Blind said.

Llantor, the first-time starter, was in a state of terror. He was a huge bay. The wide steel apparatus that was the starting gate was obviously to him an awesome specter. He was familiar with it, having been trained from it since his earliest days — in his first year he was taught to stand in it, in his second year to break from it — but never before had he been asked to approach it and leave it as part of a group, amid all the excitement, the shouting, the bustling. So he was suspicious and fearful of the starting gate and of the other horses already in their starting stalls, who were suddenly his enemies. Each time he was advanced to his stall, he balked and turned away.

The assistant starter, when he had the horse's attention, tapped the steel in the inner side of the cubicle. "See," he said, "it don't hurt." He displayed his hand as proof that the contact of flesh and steel was of no danger. "See, it don't hurt me. It won't hurt you."

The assistant starter kept tapping the steel on the inside of the cubicle and kept showing his hand. The part he was tapping was bent and misshapen. It was in that condition from the thousands of horses that had bumped their hinds against it, sometimes bumping, savagely, the riders and assistant starters with them.

Edward Blind now had ten seconds to get his horses in, if he was to get them out on time. For a starter there was great pride in getting his horses out on time. Of equal importance was getting them out evenly, all in the same state of readiness. If some horses were up off their feet, their heads to a side, the field would break unevenly, the advantage going to the horses that were planted on all fours, head looking straight down the track. Of no less importance was getting everybody off safely. The longer the horses were in their stalls, closed up from behind and front, the more chance there was of injury.

"Back him up," Edward Blind instructed.

The horse was led to his stall hind first. He was then quickly turned about and before he had a chance to protest, was in his stall.

"Okay, let's get the one," Edward Blind said.

Ravenous, Blum's mount, saved for last because he had been unruly in the gate in his most recent outing, was not the problem he was expected to be. In fact, he got into the gate rather calmly and as a reward Blum patted him on the neck, once they were closed in.

In his right hand Edward Blind gripped the electric nozzle that controlled the giant twelve-cell batteries on either side of the starting gate.

From his perch the view was of nine horses, nine riders, evenly aligned.

The horses, jouncing back and forth — even butting the front doors — swaying side to side, shifting feet, were coiled for action. The faces of the riders were so contorted from concentration that they all appeared to be smiling.

Edward Blind, sensing the moment, the exact split second when it was all together and right, the moment that would never come again, pressed his thumb vigorously on the button of the nozzle. The doors flung open, the horses lunged, free. The riders, throwing up the leather, cried, "Yaaaah!" and way upstairs, roof level, Bob Weems, the announcer, exclaimed, "They're off!"

Not far from Bob Weems, on his own balcony, Sam Boulmetis, binoculars to his eyes, headset earphones to his ears, saw the field break evenly. From so high and complete a view, the horses, now in the first phase of the race, gave the general impression of being automatons linked irrevocably by invisible chains, the fate of each in the hands of an amused satyr who from his Olympian heights manipulated the earthly figures to conform to a preordained — or whimsical — scheme.

Leaving the starting gate, the anthropomorphic figures arranged and rearranged themselves in dreamlike patterns and sequences, continuing to do so the remainder of the way. Along the first eighth of a mile they were haphazardly wide and far apart.

In the next furlong the field apportioned itself thin at the vertex, wide at the base. In coming to the corner the field drew in from the width and the length, giving, as it went around the corner, the illusion of being a single unit operating on thirty-six legs. On the turn the field loosened up again, going wide. Coming around to the final straightaway it serried again.

"Lookin' good." The message, coming through Sam Boulmetis' earphones, crackled. The preceding patrol judges had likewise reported: "Lookin' good." To a lesser degree, Sam Boulmetis could see that much for himself. He discerned no infractions, such as excessive bumping in close quarters, that would warrant an inquiry. There was some bumping, but a certain amount had to be allowed. When they came in close together, each rider looking for his place along the rail, making it seem that the ground had tipped to a side, a certain amount of bumping was to be expected. A steward's perspicacity was tested most severely when one horse came on and blocked the understood lane of another. Had he impeded the progress of a running horse or one that was falling back anyhow?

Indoors, in the small room, Richard Lawrenson, standing in front of the closed-circuit television, getting the close-up picture, also was pleased with the shape the race was taking. His view was of horses coming straight on. When the video lost the forward motion and began showing the view from the rear, Lawrenson flicked a switch and picked up a new camera, although the rear visual was no less valuable.

With the overhead rear shot, he could see if any rider was using his whip against another rider. None was.

From the rear he could see if a rider who seemed to be whipping his horse actually was whipping him. Sometimes a rider gave the appearance of whipping his horse when really he was making no contact. This was done when the jockey did not want his horse to win for one reason or another. If this came to the attention of the steward, the jockey would be set down for "failure to persevere with his mount," the fancy term for stiffing. The head-on view gave the steward another perspective from which to judge stiffing.

The best way to stiff a horse was to keep his head down — a subtle business, so subtle, in fact, that many stewards are not even aware of it as a method.

Sam Boulmetis was, but, as the field left the quarter pole as a pack and straightened out for the dash home, he saw nothing of it; what he did see was one horse leave the pack as though it had been cast: Ravenous.

As Ravenous came within inches of the finish wire, the two Jones Precision cameras, located in a room several doors to the right of where Sam Boulmetis was standing, were being set for operation, John Penta, the cameraman, in attendance. The use of two cameras is standard, in case one goes bad. The results are photographed on 35mm film. On the bottom and on the top of the print are aligned numbers, bisected by the finish wire, and these aligned numbers rotate in succession. As each horse approaches the wire he is photographed in alignment with the wire and the correlated numbers. The film, when developed (usually within 15 seconds of the completion of a race), will show the horse in his position of finish, the name of the track, the date, and at the upper tip the view as reflected by the mirror stationed by the wire — in case an outside horse blocks the view of a horse on the inside.

As Ravenous came within a fraction of the finish line, John Penta set his cameras to work. The lens focused on Ravenous and, as they came within range, the horses that made up the rest of the field, one by one. The first horse of the rest of the field was ten lengths behind — hardly a photo finish.

As Ravenous crossed the wire, Sam Boulmetis removed his earphones and heard, for the first time since the start of the race, the roar of the crowd.

While the riders went upfield, riding out their horses, Sam Boulmetis and Keene Daingerfield stepped back indoors. The three stewards nodded, in agreement that no infractions had been evident. The word was relayed next door, to the placing judges, who had, in the meantime, received and studied the print of the race. One of the placing judges then flicked a switch that on the Tote Board in the infield registered the number one next to the number one, under the heading Results. Another roar went up.

Had either, or all, of the three stewards noticed an infraction, the Inquiry sign would immediately have been flashed. The stewards would rerun the race (as they would anyhow), observing the questionable phase closely. If, in the end, they fell short of a unanimous verdict, the majority view would hold. No decision was final, however, until the accountable rider had had a chance to tell his side of the story, which he did by means of the telephone in the tunnel.

Now Sam Boulmetis went back onto the balcony and observed, immediately below him, the riders dismounting. After they dismounted they weighed out with their equipment, under the watchful eye of Tom Kelly, clerk of scales. The riders were expected to do the same weight coming back as coming in, though on hot days they were allowed a two to three pound difference. Some riders lost as much as eight pounds in a race on a hot day.

All the riders were weighed out. Each rider, after weighing out, handed his equipment to his valet and disappeared into the tunnel. Approaching the winner's circle Walter Blum was greeted with cheers and boos. Before he went into the winner's circle he stepped on the scale. When he stepped off, Tom Kelly waved his program up in the direction of Sam Boulmetis. Sam Boulmetis waved back, and Blum's 3,999th win was official.

Chapter 24

At about the same time, over at Liberty Bell Racetrack in Philadelphia, a rider of comparable abilities was not having it so good. Bill Tichenor had at one time been considered as good a rider as Walter Blum. But in the week of Walter Blum's 4,000, Tichenor could not win a race.

"I guess you would have to say I'm dejected," Bill Tichenor said shortly after checking in with Stanley Austin, the bald, almost toothless custodian of the jockeys' room at Liberty Bell. On the desk in front of Stanley Austin was a yellow legal pad that had on it the name of every rider scheduled to ride in the afternoon, and as each rider came in his name was checked off. This was usually the job of Frank Sammarco, the clerk of scales, but Frank was at the dentist's this morning, so Stanley Austin was taking his place for the time being. He also had to note the rider's listed weight, which was marked to the right of the rider's name, and when the rider got on the scale he had to see that the figures matched. If they did not, he had to make the subtraction and give the order to go into the hotbox. He was nervous about the job. It was obvious he could do without the responsibility, and he was not as relaxed as he usually was.

It was much better for him with Frank Sammarco around. With Frank Sammarco around, he knew which way he was going and which of the outsiders who periodically visited the jockeys' room was to be liked or disliked. On his own he was not sure. It was a matter of fact that if Frank Sammarco did not like a person, Stanley Austin gave him the cold shoulder.

Stanley Austin did not have too broad a view of the outside world, having spent most of his adult years in one jockeys' room or another. He was a jockey himself in the thirties and forties and was reputed to be the rider to have broken Lucien Laurin's maiden as a trainer, though he himself claimed not to have too clear a memory of that. What he always remembered was that he was in Allentown in 1932 when three riders were killed in one spill. That he would never forget.

In front of the locker next to Bill Tichenor's a valet named Harvey was polishing a saddle and talking about a much more recent spill, one in New England, which had been fatal to Henry Wadja. Harvey spoke in a whisper when he spoke of Henry Wadja, since he did not want to spook the jockeys nearby. Henry Wadja had been a close friend of his, Harvey said, and it was a shame about him. It was a shame about every jockey who got killed and too bad that these things had to happen. He had been there in the jocks' room many times when riders came back after a race all bruised up and injured and one or two times he had seen a jockey go out and never come back. Seemed that the riders who went the longest between injuries got hurt the worst when they did fall. Maybe, Harvey said, it was because the riders who got hurt every other day got to learn how to take a fall, whereas the others were short on practice. In any event the longer a rider went without a spill the more the fear built up, as it was a case of the inevitable, a matter of sooner or later.

Bill Tichenor was now down to his shorts and rather than go right into the hotbox, he sat in front of his locker and rested. He was thirty-one years old and on his face were the remnants of freckles. His back was wide and muscular, and his arms showed the effects of pulling in the reins of some two thousand horses. The previous two years he had been the leading rider at Liberty Bell Racetrack. This year he was nowhere near leading rider. That spot was held by Donald Brumfield, a fellow Kentuckian.

"I'm just totally discouraged," Bill Tichenor said, "about everything. About racing. About being a jockey." He spoke softly and slowly, as do most people from Beaver Falls, Kentucky. "You know, being a jockey is not the life people think it is. It's not what it's cracked up to be. Like, for instance, people will see a top jockey riding around in a Caddie or something and they'll think he's something big. A big man, you know. Well, most times that jockey can't even read or write."

Bill Tichenor was bothered by the fact that he himself had gone no further than high school. He felt that persons who had no education had no class. Class was very important to him, and class was what was missing around the racetrack.

He remembered, he said, some time ago, right here at Liberty Bell, bringing a horse in lame. "Coming around the turn for home, I eased up on him. He was limping. Well, there were a few characters along the rail who must have had a bet on the horse. And they were giving me hell. They wanted me to ride the horse out. I heard one of them yell out to me, 'Hey, Tich, you're the one who should have broken his leg!' You know, that's plain common. That's common people for you."

There were common people along the backside too.

As an apprentice Bill Tichenor had been under exclusive contract to one of the largest stables in New York. The trainer of the stable used him primarily in the mornings. Only occasionally would he put him on a horse in the afternoon. He also refused to give him back his contract. This went on for five years. So the five years that are the best years of a jockey's life, Bill Tichenor sat out.

This did not make him bitter, but it also did not make him mellifluous. In fact, being indentured to a trainer is the rule for a jockey in his apprentice years. (This rule, which in effect makes slaves of aspiring jockeys, has been lifted in some — enlightened — states.) What varies is the degree to which it is carried out. Nonetheless, the trainer actually owns his apprentice and can do with him as he pleases, and the apprentice unlucky enough to fall into the hands of an inconsiderate baron can have his career stopped before it gets started.

Bill Tichenor smiled. "I just got a letter from home. Last week they had a rocking chair contest. That's right. A rocking chair contest. That was, they tell me, the biggest thing to happen in Beaver Falls in years. Simple pleasures, right? But to me that's what life is all about. If I could go back to that kind of life, I would. But I can't. Not now." He laughed. "You know who won that rocking chair contest? My cousin."

Bill Tichenor was the second of eight children. His father was a farmer and a coal miner. The farming was not enough to put bread on the table, so he worked the mines too: a rough but satisfying life. For Bill Tichenor there is nothing like being out in the country, among friends, where one has a sense of belonging.

But the money is in the big city, more or less. The previous year Bill Tichenor earned about $85,000. "On paper it looks good. But when you subtract the fee for your valet, taxes, and a thousand other expenses, you're not left with much. Last year I was left with $30,000. That's not bad. But I don't know if it's worth the trouble."

When Bill Tichenor was finally released from his contract and became, at last, his own man, he tied up with trainer Marty Fallon, and under Fallon he did well. He got good mounts, and when you get good mounts, you win, and when you win, you get more good mounts. Then Tichenor got hurt, was out for some two months, and lost his connection with Fallon, who in the meantime found another boy. So now Tichenor was getting mounts at random. He was getting the mounts riders like Donald Brumfield refused to ride. Naturally these were the losers. So the vicious cycle went around in reverse.

"If I had it to do over again," he said, "I would still become a jockey, because of my size. But I wouldn't want my son to be a jockey."

Half the horses a rider rides are sore. Any one of these horses can fall and kill a rider.

Bill Tichenor slung a towel over his shoulder. He walked over to the bulletin board in the front of the room and looked over the program, to see what horses he would be riding in the afternoon. His best shot was on a two-year-old filly named Hickets, in a race that had five contestants.

Bill Tichenor chuckled sarcastically. "Maybe I'll even win one today," he said. He headed for the hotbox. "A jockey is always looking for that hot streak. That's the one thing that keeps me going. Today, tomorrow, I might win one and everything will be different."

He drew a deep breath as though gathering himself for a new attitude. "Don't mind me," he said, "I'm just in a lousy mood now. That's how it is when you go a whole week without a win. Last week I won seven and I was fine. Who knows? Maybe I'll win three today and that'll get me started on a hot streak. The next morning they'll be waiting for me in line. Right now I'd settle for just one win. Nothing like a win to perk you up and make the whole world look different."

The apprentice Pete Fantini was having breakfast in what passed for the recreation room — it had a Ping-Pong table (Menotte Aristone was playing Ping-Pong with a fellow named Lucky). The recreation room was shabby and small; six or seven stools and a counter made up the dining area. Standing behind the counter, reading *Jane Eyre*, was the cook and waiter, Steve, a college student. He did his reading of *Jane Eyre* in between the cooking and the serving. He was now serving John Baboolal, the rider from Trinidad.

John Baboolal had a limitless appetite. He would run up to the counter and ask for a hamburger, gulp it down, run out again, come back, ask for another hamburger, then soup, then another hamburger, and in a period of a half hour consume something like fourteen hamburgers and twelve bowls of soup. Where he ran off to after each ingestion was a mystery, but it is safe to assume that he was in some quiet corner passing it all up.

Pete Fantini was having eggs sunny side up, toast, and orange juice. He said he could eat all he wanted to this morning as his weight was down to 102, where it was required to be 104. The eggs, the toast, and the orange juice were worth two pounds. That's how he ate: by the pound.

"I'm having a real good meet," he said, "and being an apprentice don't bother me. I can ride with the best of them."

He was now a one-bug apprentice, at age twenty-one. He was under contract to the same trainer who had let go of Bill Tichenor. Under Marty Fallon, Pete Fantini was getting the mounts Bill Tichenor used to get. So that for this meeting he was second in the leading rider standings with, so far, thirty-nine firsts, twenty-seven seconds, and twenty-nine thirds. Pete Fantini was flushed with confidence.

"I'm going to make a lot of money. I got the most successful trainer behind me, and I'm doing good for him. I used to have trouble getting out of the gate when I first started. You know, I'd break before my horse. But I got that straightened out and the guy that helped me a lot there was Danny Perlsweig. He took his time with me and he taught me how to relax going into the gate and now when I go into the gate I'm relaxed. I'm still no Walter Blum. He's the best gate man there is. But I'm good."

There was no question that Pete Fantini was good, but since he was an apprentice, there was a question as to how long he would be good. This, however, was not a matter of concern to Pete Fantini at the moment. He was certain that he would be as good in twenty years as he was now, that the bountiful years were all ahead. One could not blame Pete Fantini for being so right within himself: he was indeed young and talented, quite the sensation at Liberty Bell Racetrack. What's more, he had got in solid with a trainer of fine horses, and there was every reason to believe that this relationship would endure. At least that's what Pete Fantini believed.

Getting in good with a trainer, he said, was most important to a jockey. He had been lucky that way. He felt sorry, he said, for the jockeys who had not been as lucky as he.

But, he said, you cannot feel sorry for everybody.

Bill Tichenor won his race that afternoon, on Hickets, in the rain and mud. Before the race the jockeys protested about having to go out. Then they went out and raced before empty stands. Everybody was inside. The horses and their riders splashing around the oval, slowly and heavily, made dark, muddy figures. Since it all took place before stands that were empty and supporters who were not there, the scene had the quality of a fantasy, as though it were all happening on an aphotic screen of a silent movie, in slow motion.

Moments after the race Bill Tichenor was sitting in front of his locker, almost smiling. He stared at the newspaper clipping that was pasted on his locker door. The clipping read: "Success is the freedom to do what you want when you want." Bill Tichenor said that was the ideal he strove for.

Chapter 25

Moments after Walter Blum won the first race of the afternoon (with such ease), Jim Raftery was in the bright, sunlit publicity office cleaning off the gigantic "4,000" sign. The background of the sign was white, the lettering red. From being left around the past few days, the sign had collected some dirt. Jim Raftery used a moist rag to erase smudges. "I feel it in my bones," he said, the cameras dangling from his neck.

Blum's mount in the second race was the three-year-old filly, Angel Clipper. The week before, in similar company, Manuel Cedeno had brought Angel Clipper in first, by a head. If Manuel Cedeno could bring the horse in first, think what Walter Blum could do!

"What a great guy for it to happen to and what a great day for it to happen on," Jim Raftery said.

Being a photographer, Jim Raftery was very conscious of the weather. What rotten luck if Blum should win his 4,000th on a cloudy day.

Jane Goldstein, the assistant publicity director, an attractive brunette, was watching Jim Raftery polish off the sign and, at the same time, handing out press releases that had Blum's 4,000th win as accomplished fact. "This is very good for racing," she said.

Jane Goldstein is one of the more astute publicity people. She is keenly aware that racing's good name is dependent, to varying degrees, on the relationship that exists between the front office and the press, a somewhat exceptional attitude in racing, which is generally filled with functionaries who are loud and tough rather than courteous and tactful.

"You don't think we're jinxing him, do you?" Jane Goldstein asked Jim Raftery, as she helped him remove a particularly obstinate spot on the sign.

"Naw," Jim Raftery said, finally holding up the sign in full view of everybody in the office.

"Nice," Jane Goldstein said.

"But heavy," Jim Raftery said.

He carried the heavy sign outdoors. The sun was very bright, and on the porch of the administration building a few people were fanning themselves with their programs. When they saw Jim Raftery carrying the huge sign, one said to the others, "He know something we don't know?"

As the horses were being marched through the tunnel Jim Raftery toted the bulky sign to the winner's circle, taking some kidding along the way. In the winner's circle he wearily set the sign down to lean against his legs and blew out a sigh.

A wasted effort. Michael Hole took the second race aboard Funfair, leaving Blum and Angel Clipper behind a distant fifth.

Then the Latins were heard from, and they would yet leave their mark on the day. In the microcosm of an afternoon they would signal their intentions for the next decade. In the third race, which Blum sat out, as he would the fourth, Carlos Barrera gave a display of the daring that made the Latins so portentous. At the outset of the race he was, on Title Shot, so far back that he was being ridiculed. Along the backstretch he was dead last, and that's where he was, last and on the far outside, when the field turned for home. In the last stage of the race he came on with a wild burst, weaving in and out of traffic in seeming abandon, virtually picking off horses left and right, until he found a secure place along the rail. Then, once along the rail, he pulled away nice and easy, crossing the wire a length and a half to the good of the placer. In his drive to the rail he had, of course, cut in front of horses, yet his precision was such that no rider claimed obstruction.

This was riding at its best and Carlos Barrera, a hot and cold rider if there ever was one, was at his most effective.

The Latin Humberto Aguilera, aboard Concologist, won the next race in far more leisurely fashion, taking an early lead and holding it all the way to the finish, threatened only slightly along the stretch by the fast-closing Painted Beauty, ridden by Vincent Bracciale, Jr., who was having one of his poorer afternoons.

For the Americans, it was getting to be that kind of a day.

Chapter 26

Pete Mikos had watched the third race on the firehouse television. The backside was now very hot despite the trees, and the soil was crusty. Outside the firehouse people and horses moved about slowly and languidly. Inside the firehouse the firemen, shirttails hanging out, mopped their brows. Pete Mikos was in his jeans and sweatshirt — his biceps clearly showing — watching the third race from the first row of collapsible chairs. Behind him were six more rows of collapsible chairs, all of them occupied when the horses went to post. When the horses left the gate, the firemen yelled at the television. The guards, who were supposed to be protecting the backside from intruders but were instead in the firehouse, likewise yelled at the television. Pete Mikos sat quietly. He had no bet on the race but was interested in its outcome on account of a tip he had had on Title Shot and because he was always interested in Carlos Barrera. He smiled a knowing smile when Carlos Barrera and Title Shot crossed the finish line first. Then he rushed out of the firehouse, made an abrupt right, and was in his shed row.

In the shed row all the horses were in their stalls except for

Good Hand, who was in the grazing area being prepared for the fifth race. Aloysius, his groom, was brushing him down, trying to bring out a shine on his coat. Pete Mikos went to his knees and began unfurling Good Hand's foreleg bandages.

Pete Mikos laughed. "Why're you in such a lousy mood?" he said to Aloysius. "I know you when you're wrong."

Aloysius shrugged and kept on trying to bring a shine out on the horse. No shine was coming out, and that was bad. Aloysius stepped back, put his hands to his hips, and shook his head. No shine. What's more, the horse was not dappled out. Dapples on a horse were a sure sign of fitness. Some horses did not need to glow and dapple out to be fit. Good Hand (Handy, to his friends) did.

Pete Mikos, sensing Aloysius' despair, said, "Come on, Aloysius, it's gonna be all right. We're gonna win this one. Shit, you ought to be excited and all. I mean Blum's gonna win his 4,000th on your horse. There's gonna be stories all over the country about Blum, about Handy, and about you." Pete got to his feet to see what effect he was having on Aloysius. Aloysius was still unhappy. "Your name's gonna be in every paper in the country," Pete said. "You gonna talk to us when you're famous?"

"They ain't gonna have my name in the papers," Aloysius said. "They never say nothin' about the groom. He don't exist to them."

Pete Mikos was back down on his knees. "That's right," he said. "The groom does all the work, and nobody knows he exists."

"The groom," said Aloysius, "mucks out the stalls and does all the dirty work and when the horse is sick he stays up all night with him and when he win, do you ever see the groom's picture or name in the paper? I never did."

"I never did either. But this time you'll be in. You'll be famous."

"I just want what's good for Handy."

"Listen, being Blum's 4,000th winner is good for Handy. It's good for you, too."

Aloysius mumbled something. He kept scrubbing his horse. He patted the horse on the face now and then.

"Someday," Pete laughed, "you'll be sitting around and you'll be telling stories about how you were the groom for Blum's 4,000th winner. Boy . . ." He shook his head in mock envy. Though much the younger, Pete was protective of Aloysius who, because of his bulky frame, shuffled gait, and speech impediment, gave the impression of being slow of mind. In fact — and Pete would be the first to point this out — he was a man of high intelligence, known for the provocative missives he dispatched to the newspapers on subjects ranging from horse racing to religion. As for Pete, his youth and love of life made him a man of high spirits. He was good-looking, and with that quality came a certain freedom and mastery over others. "You're excited, aren't you?" Pete said. "Come on, admit you're excited."

"I don't know."

Aloysius studied the horse's comportment.

"Something ain't right," he said. "I don't feel confident. I don't feel it in me, you know?"

Except for his dull coat, Good Hand had the presence of a champion. The thighs were muscular, the chest wide and protruding, and, perhaps most important, the high points of the back — the croup at the hind, the withers at the fore — were of equal height.

Pete was now finished with one leg, and with the dressing off he ran his hand over the ankle. "Nothing wrong with you," he said to the horse. Overnight the horse had stood in leg paint — Phenal Iodine Glicorine, known simply as PIG paint — to tighten the joints.

Shorty, who had been studying Good Hand from a source perhaps more reliable than the horse itself, the *Daily Racing Form*, joined the party around Good Hand, sucked meditatively on a strip of straw, and said, "Why do you suppose Perlsweig's putting him on the turf?"

Good Hand had never before raced on the grass.

Pete Mikos threw up his hands in resignation. "Don't ask me," he said. "Ask Danny."

"I already did."

"What did he tell you?"

"He told me it was his own fuckin' business."

Pete laughed.

"Yup," Shorty said, chomping on the straw. "That's what he

told me."

"Well," Pete said, "he's the boss."

"He's the boss all right. He's got the money."

"Shorty," Pete said, "you're so fulla money you stink from it."

"Yeah, bet your ass."

Shorty kicked some dirt and walked away, back to his lounge chair outside the room he shared with Aloysius.

"Who's got more money," Pete asked Aloysius, "you or Shorty?"

Aloysius was in no mood for light banter.

"I dunno why he's putting him on the grass," he said. "He didn't even give him a work on the grass. How are we supposed to know if he's any good on the grass?"

"We'll find out soon enough," Pete said.

Horsemen are divided along the middle on the question of what anatomical features distinguished a dirt horse from a grass horse. Some say a horse with a long pastern is the ideal grass horse. Some say a horse with a short pastern is the ideal grass horse. Take your choice.

Shorty now came back to the center of activity, slapping the *Daily Racing Form* against a leg. "Another thing," he said. "Why the hell is he putting him in a route?"

"Don't ask me," said Pete.

"I mean this horse can't do a mile and sixteenth. I can tell you that right now. That's right, I can tell you that right now." He chuckled. "No sense in even taking the horse out there, 'cause I'm telling you right now what's gonna happen. He's gonna get out in front and he's gonna tire and he ain't gonna be in sight around the turn for home. You remember what I'm telling you." Shorty was amused with himself, his eyes sparkled and his mouth with the straw in it worked fast. "Why last week he come in third, in a sprint! He couldn't last in a sprint!"

Pete Mikos asked to see Shorty's paper. Even though he had seen Handy's last race, the paper was the final word. The chart showed that in his last race — three quarters of a mile — Good Hand had been a closeup third all the way, until the last panel, where, as he was drawing to within a neck of the leader, he fell back and finished behind by a length. Still, the pace and the final time (22,

25-1/5, and 1:11) had been quite fast and a horse unable to keep up to the very end could be excused. What's more, to be among the pacesetters and finish so close to the front in that kind of a race was an indication of tenacity and a sign that a horse was rounding to peak form.

"He shows me a lot of heart," Pete said.

"I ain't arguing his heart," Shorty said. "I'm just saying he's perfectly sharpened for a sprint, so why the hell put him in a route? And on the grass. You figure that one out for me, will ya? In fact, you tell me what the fuck makes these trainers tick in the first place?"

Shorty often said that some horses won only because they overcame their training.

Pete usually enjoyed listening to Shorty. Beneath the abuse — much of it for humorous effect — there was information of great value. There was always something to be learned from Shorty. But this was not the time.

"Come on," Pete said, "you're getting Aloysius all shook up."

Aloysius, still brushing the horse down, was alternately muttering to himself and pouting.

Shorty was persistent. "I'm just trying to say what's good," he said. "I was out there this morning and I walked on the grass and it was all chopped up, coming apart. Know what I mean? That could be dangerous. I mean I wouldn't be in the least surprised if Handy come back lame."

Aloysius, now truly upset, walked away shaking his head, leaving Pete to finish the work on Good Hand. Aloysius was so deeply attached to his horses that he could not take the thought of their getting hurt. He did indeed stay up nights with them when they were sick. When, later he quit Danny Perlsweig, for reasons he said were personal, he called up every other night to find out how his horses were doing. His horses, he was told more often than not, were not doing well. They missed him, and because they missed him and his touch they were sulking and not eating and, as a consequence, running poorly. This was not altogether unusual. Mr. Correlation, as a rule the best doer of any of Danny Perlsweig's horses, stayed off his feed and was most cantankerous in the days that followed *his* groom's departure. So there was no belittling the importance of the bond that tied the horse to his groom and the groom to his horse.

Now it was time to take Good Hand out to the paddock.

"You coming?" Pete asked Aloysius.

Aloysius said he was not coming. Pete did not press the issue. It was better actually that he did not go out with the horse. In the paddock during the saddling a nervous groom was a danger to the horse. He would transmit his tightness to the horse and spook him. Pete then asked Aloysius if he was at least coming out later on to watch the race from the grandstand with the rest of them. Aloysius said, no. Didn't he want to be there when his horse made history? Not really. He was not that interested. Then for certain he would watch the race from the firehouse television? No, Aloysius said. He had things to do.

In the walking ring out front Shorty walked Good Hand around. He was careful not to get his horse too close to the horse in front. He kept his own head up. A few days before he had kept his head down and marched his horse straight into the rear and into the hind legs of a horse in front, causing his horse to throw a shoe and be scratched. Danny Perlsweig had not been very pleased. Pete Mikos stood under a tree with Danny Perlsweig watching Shorty and Good Hand go around. Pete was watching how careful Shorty was being. He smiled at Shorty. Shorty knew what the smile was all about.

Then the riders came out and joined their owners and trainers. Miguel Rivera, who was to ride a twenty-five to one shot, Blaze Tyson, kept thwacking his whip against his white pants as he took instructions; Vincent Bracciale, Jr., had the look of disinterest common to the precocious; Carlos Barrera kept nodding and smiling as though too eager to please; Michael Hole, as always, seemed impatient and perturbed. There were now, in all, ten riders in the paddock.

The center of attention, of course, was Walter Blum. Every move was followed closely. As he listened to Danny Perlsweig his arms were folded over his chest, the whip dangling loosely in front of him. Blum nodded, then smiled, then frowned, always squinting when his eyes met the sun, especially on the right side. The spectators around the fence of the circle were for the most part friendly, many of them offering words of encouragement. An exception was one fellow in a crew cut who bellowed, "You fuckin' pygmy!" Blum, obviously not deaf to the taunt, remained unmoved. Dave Hart, one of the more interested spectators, winced.

Blum was saying to Danny Perlsweig, "This horse never ran on the grass before, did he?"

"No, he hasn't, Walter, but his sire and dam were fine grass horses, so I expect him to run a good race."

Blum, chewing hard on the gum in his mouth, nodded. The gum chewing made him appear casual and carefree, conveying insouciance. Any pressures or tensions he felt before a race of whatever importance were deeply reserved within him. Through the years, as a public figure, he had learned to present a front of inscrutability. (Chewing gum, however, served an important function as a moistener, taking the place of the water he could not imbibe in order to do his weight.)

"This horse likes to go to the front," Danny Perlsweig said, "so don't fight him too much."

"Okay."

"Get him warmed up first, then try to lay around third or fourth with him."

"I'll try not to let him out too much."

"That's right. Try to lay around third or fourth with him, then you should be able to open him up."

Danny Perlsweig boosted Blum on the horse. On the horse, Blum, tugging the reins, getting the feel of the horse, said, "I'll do my best." He patted Good Hand on the crest. He had ridden him in the spring but needed reacquainting. So he patted the horse and whispered in his ear.

When the horses went postward, Pete Mikos and his friends stood by the rail in the grandstand near the finish line and the tunnel. Pete Mikos had bought a hot dog and was eating it with great appetite. He wiped the corners of his mouth and said, "Handy was all broke out in the paddock. I wonder what that means."

Lou Goldberg, the groom Pete Mikos was still breaking in, said, "Isn't it natural for a horse to sweat when it's so hot?"

Pete said, "Not always. To every horse it means something different. For Handy I don't know what it means."

What it meant for Handy was that he was not fit. He did not run a good race; in fact, he ran the race Shorty had predicted to the extent that he came back sore. Blum had obviously been unable to rate the horse and so had let him take the early lead. The pace he set exhausted him for the finish. He finished sixth. Blaze Tyson, Miguel Rivera up, finished first. Three straight for the Latins.

When Blum dismounted, he explained to Danny Perlsweig that the horse had simply tired.

Pete Mikos and Lou Goldberg and the vindicated Shorty now walked Good Hand past the grandstand on the way to the backside. Along the grandstand thousands of losing tickets floated to the ground.

Shorty walked with his head down, rolling a strip of straw around in his mouth. He shook his head. He said Blum had given the horse a bad ride. Why had Blum let him get out that fast? Didn't he know the horse needed to be rated? If the horse had been rated, maybe he would not have won, but there was a good chance he would have been someplace on the board — third, maybe even second. He had shown life, the horse. You could never tell with jockeys, Shorty said. Pete Mikos said, "That's for sure."

The freshness in Pete Mikos was gone. He was exhausted and dispirited, like the horse he was guiding back to the shed row. The area above the horse's left hind hoof was bleeding. The coronet and the pastern had taken a bearing on the turf. Maybe it was the rider's fault. Pete said that some riders always brought their horses back all bloodied up. Blum was not that kind of a rider, but maybe this time he had done something wrong.

He should have rated him better, Shorty said.

As Pete, Shorty, and Good Hand passed the far end of the grandstand, the spectators who had no reason to go inside and watch the rerun watched them. One of the spectators had an especially vacant look in his eyes. He was sitting way up in the back rows of the grandstand, slumped in his seat, hidden from view. Pete Mikos had gained an accidental glimpse of this distant, hulking figure, but he never let on that he had seen Aloysius.

Chapter 27

The exhibition race, which was run between the seventh and the eighth, under a clear bright sky, reaffirmed the maxim that a rider is only as good as his horse. In this case Walter Blum was not as good as Baeza's Linda's Chief.

Exhibition races or match races can be very exciting or very dull. This one, if suspense was the criterion, was dull. The outcome was never in doubt, for Linda's Chief drew away farther and farther from his main rival, Impecunious, with every stride, and it was plain, at least on this day, in this race, that Linda's Chief was far the superior horse.

Naturally on mounts so inequitable in talent, it was impossible to make judgments on the worth of one rider over another, but it was interesting to perceive the difference in styles and to notice that the great riders were not imprisoned by one particular style. Blum, known as the pumping jockey, and Baeza, known as the jockey who sat still on his horses, exchanged roles, Baeza going all out from the start, pumping away, and Blum sitting still and not making a move until the far turn — to no avail, as it developed.

So what was supposed to be a race for the entertainment of the public turned out to be an event for the insiders, the serious students of horsemanship. Watching the race with unusual interest were the young tyros — among others John Mallano — and the old soldiers. Isaias Martinez, of the latter, was so absorbed in the details of Baeza's performance that at one point he let his broom fall from his grasp.

Here was Ycaza's inheritor. The significance of the race aside — as a race it really had no meaning — here was the preeminent Latin engaging the dominant American, and if the terms were not equal, well, that made it all the more boding: it testified to the hardening truth that if on any given day, on any given track, the best American was as good as the best Latin, the Latin would be on the better horse.

Quite simply, nobody in the country was winning more money than Velasquez, Pincay, and Baeza, and nobody was better. They came no better than Velasquez, the young, cheerful, curly haired Panamanian who at the concurrent Saratoga meeting was winning one stakes after another. In stakes races alone he finished the meeting with a total of $152,145. Donald MacBeth joked: "The horses are running so fast for you they're blowing your hair off." (Velasquez was beginning to go bald up front.) Or Pincay, the Panamanian with the pitch black hair, baby-smooth complexion, who, in his mid-twenties, was into his fourth year as leading money rider in the country. Indeed, by the end of the year he was to reach and exceed the unprecedented four million dollar mark. And Baeza, now the most selective of the three, who, since the mid-sixties, was the most consistent money rider of them all.

Yet to voice the assertion that nobody was better than these three Latins could, along certain parts of the backstretch, get you a very respectable black eye. You mean Arcaro wasn't better? Was there ever a man — is there a man — who could rate his horse like Arcaro? And Shoemaker. Even now, who had his "touch," his feel? Whose hands were as light? And then what about Blum?

Blum, of course, is a special case because while he is certainly the best there is in getting out of the gate and getting to the front, he is nothing to bet the house and furniture on when it comes to bringing a horse from behind, from off the pace. His weakness is rating.

At least that is his reputation (speed horse, get Blum), and yet some of his finest triumphs have come aboard horses who had to be brought from behind. The quintessential example of this was the 1971 Belmont.

On the afternoon of the 1971 Belmont, Blum's mount, Pass Catcher, was paid scant attention and went off at very high odds. This was, in fact, an oversight because Pass Catcher, Blum up, had come close to winning the recent mile-and-an-eighth Jersey Derby at Garden State, losing the race by a charging neck in an effort that seemed a sure sharpener for the more strenuous mile-and-a-half Belmont. But the betting public had its attention diverted by that year's sensation, the Venezuelan Canonero II, who had won the two earlier three-year-old classics, the Kentucky Derby and the Preakness — the Kentucky Derby in a smashing come-from-behind effort, the Preakness in front-running style — and was now surely going to make a joke of the Belmont and win for himself the elusive Triple Crown.

Now if a rider's ability to rate a horse was ever tested it was surely in a mile and a half event. Rare was the three-year-old who could skip out front and last the distance. So right from the start Blum lay fourth, letting Canonero II and two others set the pace. Even during the race itself the crowd overlooked Pass Catcher. Indeed, with a machine (as Blum referred to Canonero II) leading the way, fourth did not seem a threatening spot, especially when occupied by a horse with comparatively meager credentials and a rider known primarily for his front-running artistry.

So the crowd took no notice when at the half-mile pole Blum let the reins out a notch and moved Pass Catcher effortlessly from fourth to third along the rail, or even when, swinging around the far turn, hugging the rail to save ground, he moved him nice and gradually from third to second.

At this phase, in coming to the quarter pole, Blum knew he had the race and was on his way to one of the biggest upsets of the decade, not to mention a gratifying personal "milestone." He later recalled: "I could sense I was going to beat Canonero because by the quarter pole I could see he was under a pretty good drive, while I felt a lot of horse under me. Sometimes you just know when your horse has got what it takes. It's like a quarterback when he throws a pass. As soon as the ball leaves his hand, he knows if his man's going to catch it. When a golfer hits a golf ball, he knows as soon as he hits it if he hit it right. Same with a rider. When you ride a horse that's running, when you've got a lot of horse under you, you feel a lot of animal under you. He doesn't feel loose and weak and not willing. You just feel like he's a tiger. When a horse is like that, I don't care who he's up against, he's liable to do anything."

With a quarter of a mile to go the crowd finally took notice of Pass Catcher. He boldly drew up to Canonero II, then passed him, and went on to win by four lengths.

What it proved was that Pass Catcher was a fine horse and that Walter Blum was a jockey who could rate.

Could he rate his horses as well as Braulio Baeza? The answer is yes, even if to the untrained eye it does not always seem that way, for it is far easier to conclude that a horse is being rated when he comes from off the pace than when he sets it, and yet it takes as much rating and pacing to keep a horse up front as it takes to bring him from behind. A mediocre rider can get the horse out front, but only a gifted rider can keep him in front all the way, setting a false pace, appearing to go all out when in fact he is saving his horse. Rating him, in other words. And this is Blum's genius. This skill is what sets him apart.

Rating a horse is no simple task. It is much like riding a car with not quite enough gas to get you to the nearest gas station. Just what do you do? Do you stay at an even speed? If you do that, you will likely come up short. Should you then gun it at the start, consume all your gas early in the going, but build up enough momentum to be able to coast on neutral the rest of the way? Or would it be wiser to start off slowly, save on the gas, coast where you can, and hope to have enough gas left over for a big rush at the end?

Blum prefers the heavy-footed start — if deceptively so. Baeza is a gas-saver. Yet as was demonstrated in the exhibition race, when the situation demanded it both men are resourceful enough to take the other's approach. So for the serious student of horsemanship the Baeza/Blum contest was indeed instructive.

Except perhaps to Walter Blum who is happier when he wins than when he gives lessons. "I don't go out there to put on a show," he said before the race. "I go out there to win."

The question was: Does a minor race mean much to you? Of course it means much to him. Because for Walter Blum there are no small challenges. In approaching anything competitive, he is downright grim. He is used to winning and does not like to lose, and that attitude extends even to leisure activities: golf, tennis, softball, even Ping-Pong.

Once when he lost a friendly game of Ping-Pong to a newspaper reporter, the sting of defeat was plain on his face. He did not throw a temper tantrum, or behave rudely, but it was obvious that he did not like the kidding that followed defeat in so meaningless a game as Ping-Pong. But then nothing was meaningless that in the end would produce a winner and a loser.

So when the great Panamanian Braulio Baeza encroached on his territory and posed a challenge, Blum was not likely to pass the matter over with a shrug. He had too big an ego for that. Monmouth, after all, was his domain. The entire New Jersey circuit was his domain. He was king at Garden State, Monmouth, Atlantic City — and sometimes Florida and California. (The Florida Turf Writers Association voted him Florida's outstanding jockey for 1972-73.) Then, too, there was the ever-present teaser — were the New York jockeys really the best? Of course this was the same as asking, were the Panamanians really the best, for the best jockeys in New York were the Panamanians.

Actually the confrontation between the two began in the jockeys' room. When Braulio Baeza reported in about an hour before the race, Blum and he shook hands, exchanged friendly greetings, and all the while stared at each other like two boxers in the ring before a championship match. What was evident throughout the brief encounter was the respect the other jockeys in the room had for both of them. While they were talking, none of the other riders made a move to join the conversation. Only after they broke off and went their separate ways, each man to his own locker, did some of the others circle around Baeza, and then not for long, for Baeza was not given to jocularity. His face, with the droopy eyelids, the pronounced cheekbones, was a mask of impassivity. It was as though he were a hired hand, come to do just another job, to dispose of just one more enemy.

What's more, he would not undress in front of an audience. Neither would Walter Blum. In the jockeys' room it was not unusual to find various jockeys walking around completely naked — and that was all right, that was the way it was in all locker rooms. But Blum and Baeza had an inherent sense of propriety that would not permit that. Quality in a man shows in small ways. Interestingly the higher you get in the ranks of jockeys, the higher the quality. When you meet the Shoemakers, the Arcaros, the Baezas, the Blums, there is no mistaking the excellence of character. They are gentlemen. They may lack formal education, but the years give them a fine smoothness — and, of course, success has a way of building character, or is it character that breeds success?

When you go down in the ranks, it does not necessarily follow that you are dealing with louts, but that you are dealing with men who are, to be generous, unworldly. This, in some cases, yields a preference for booze, drugs, and language that is not tolerated outside the backstretch or the jockeys' room. Of such, indeed, are the jockeys who use the batteries, the joints, on their horses, when they can get away with it — on the average only one horse out of ten responds favorably to a battery — because to them that is the ticket to survival. The Blums and Baezas will not go near a battery because of self-esteem and because they have learned that in relating to owners and trainers charm is equal in importance to talent and that an agreeable nature gets you further than a battery. As Blum says: "Trainers and owners don't like no wise guys."

So on this very hot, sunny afternoon were the two leading riders of the day, one the Latin, the other the American, and they were expected to settle once and for all the question of supremacy and all they proved was that today Linda's Chief was better than Impecunious.

That's why they called it horse racing.

Friday Morning

Chapter 28

By 7:30 Walter Blum was in the track kitchen sipping his coffee and reading his *Daily Racing Form.* Around him other jockeys were doing pretty much the same, except for Menotte Aristone, in for the day from Liberty Bell, who was moving from table to table spreading his good humor and leaving everybody laughing. Menotte had a happy-go-lucky style and was always grinning. The man appeared to have no problems. In a way that was so. His father was a millionaire, and that was something to grin about. Then too, the past year he'd had considerable success in stakes on Real Note and various other horses, all of them trained by Ben Perkins, the trainer he rode for to the virtual exclusion of others. On the other hand, the previous spring at Garden State all of Ben Perkins' horses had been destroyed in a fire and for a time it had seemed as if the end of Ben Perkins and Menotte Aristone had arrived.

Though Menotte came from a wealthy family, he had spent his better years riding the half-milers and the bullrings and getting very tough at it — so tough that, he admits, when he finally made it to the respectable tracks he had a hard time keeping his fists to himself, being always ready to slug it out with any rider who bothered him however slightly or unintentionally. He was no longer that way — at least not much.

Now he was concentrating on being a good rider, and his idea of a good rider was Howard Grant, from whom he had learned his most important lesson, which was this: when you are coming down the stretch, the horse beginning to tire and buckle under you, instead of whipping him you pick him up — that is, bring the reins in close and tight, picking up his head, thereby giving the horse his confidence. Otherwise, when you whip the horse, he sulks and his tail goes in between his legs. Howard Grant, according to Menotte and others, was so much the master that some riders actually stayed off the pace with him just to see what he was doing on a horse. Whatever it was he did, there was no imitating him. "There is no imitating natural ability," Menotte said.

Anyway, after Benny Perkins' horses were destroyed in the fire, Menotte's father, Roland, among others, provided the money that yielded for Perkins one champion after another, the most celebrated of which was Real Note.

When Menotte came to Blum's table — Blum and he shared the same agent — he slapped him on the back, whispered something funny in his ear, and walked out the door whistling. Blum yawned, took a sip of his coffee, and resumed reading his paper.

Blum scanned the front and the back pages — the feature pages — of the *Daily Racing Form* and stopped when he came to the story of his being one away from 4,000. He read the story and was not happy. "The facts are right," he said. "I got no quarrel with the facts. But these hundred dollar words . . ." Blum prefers five and ten dollar words, words a person can understand. A writer who wrote fancy on a paper was like a rider who rode fancy on a horse. Blum can abide neither.

Blum is put off by big words and "big shot intellectuals." For all that, he is a literate man. Most riders are not. Most riders at once fear and respect anyone who has had "schooling." Donald MacBeth, the fiery Canadian rider, once stared unbelievingly at a man who claimed to be a writer of books. He contemplated the man as though viewing an apparition. "How long do you have to go to school to be a book writer?" he finally asked. But there was the rider Rocco Gabriella who feared that in time jockeys would be the only illiterate people on earth. Soon everybody would have a Ph.D. and only jockeys would be distinct and recognizable. Gabriella: "Someday when you go to a party it'll be meet doctor this, doctor that, and nobody'll know who the hell anybody is." So perhaps there was a benefit in not pursuing an education.

When Blum was through scanning the feature pages of the *Daily Racing Form*, he turned to the inside of the paper and got serious studying the charts of the five horses he would ride in the afternoon. Of the five he had his best shot on Student Lamp in the seventh.

Done with the charts he returned to the front page and came across an item that disturbed him, a note about a horse winning a big stakes race out of town. At first, he smiled as he said: "As you can see, I wasn't on him." But suddenly he was earnest and angry. "I should have been. I won on that horse. I won on him by eighteen lengths. That was the trouble. The trainer was pissed off that I let him get out by that much. When a horse wins by that much the next time he runs they put that much more weight on him, and the trainer didn't like that."

Blum paused and lit a cigarette. He took a few drags and said, "That's the bad thing about racing. Sometimes no matter what you do is wrong. Sure I let the horse run out and if I had to do it again I would do it again because me, I never hold horses. It's against everything I believe. I got the reputation of being an honest jockey and I've maintained this thing with horsemen through the years. They know I'm not going to hold a horse.

"I mean that's a bad situation, holding horses. Most jockeys don't hold horses, but some do and why? Because they know if they don't hold them they won't ride for the guy anymore. I'm thankful I've never been in that position. My agent don't ride for guys that might want me to hold a horse.

"But there's all kinds of guys in this world. Some trainers will tell their jockeys, 'This horse is not ready today and I don't want you to abuse him. I just want you to get a good race out of him.'

See, the next time he runs he might try with him, you know, to win a big bet.

"Well, to me that's holding a horse, not asking for his whole thing. I just don't like to do that. I don't have to do it."

Blum was red in the face. The subject of holding horses stirred him and worked him up. His coffee had gone cold, but he still sipped at it.

"If you hold a horse," he said, "why eventually you get the reputation of doing that, and once you do, you might as well write yourself off. Because guys aren't going to trust you. It's okay if you're going to ride a horse and you're going to do your best on him and after you do your best you see he's not going to win; then it's okay if you don't beat him up.

"That's ridiculous, to beat him up when you know he can't win. So what you do when you know he can't win is let him continue around the racetrack and you get a good race out of him. But to go out there with the thought that you're not going to let him run, that's another thing.

"It's done, but I don't think it's commonplace. You have to face the wrath of the stewards if they catch you doing it, and they can catch you, man. Because if you ride a horse for ten thousand dollars and he finishes tenth and the next week you ride him and he finishes tenth and then the following week you run him for twelve thousand and he wins, well, the stewards are going to say, 'What the hell happened to this horse? It's a reversal of form.'

"Then they'll go back to the races you rode him in before and they'll watch the films and they'll scrutinize every inch of the film. They're not dumb. They can see if you're holding a horse or not. It's very easy to see. If they catch you, they'll suspend you, for much more than five or ten days."

Referring to one rider in particular, he said, "Now this guy just got called up for not persevering with his mount through the stretch. The stewards couldn't really prove that he held the horse. They looked at the movies, they watched him ride the horse, and they felt he did not put forth a real effort.

"But they couldn't go into court or before the Racing Commission and say he didn't put forth a real effort because he did hit his horse and did go along with him, but at the three-eighth pole he just sat still on him. So they didn't say that he held his horse. They said he had not persevered with his mount.

"What they should have said, really, if they were just going to fine him, which they did, they should have said, 'For not riding his horse out at the finish.' That doesn't sound like he held the horse.

"But not persevering with his mount, that sounds like he held the horse."

Blum lit another cigarette.

"And to top it all off," he said, "the guy had a good argument. He argued that the horse wasn't running sound. That he was choppy and sore. So he just didn't ride him anymore.

"That makes a lot of sense. But they didn't believe him. They didn't believe him because he's got a reputation. That's the problem. They would never fine me for doing that because if they did I would appeal it and I would beat it."

Blum later went out and worked a horse for Larry Jennings. The horse was a two-year-old that had never done anything in the gate but stand. Today he was being taught how to break. He would need only the one lesson.

Blum brought the horse to the gate, and as soon as the starter released the door, the horse was hustled out in a gallop. This was a totally new experience for the two-year-old. Up to now the gate had been a nice place to relax in. From this moment the gate would mean work, combat, and it will always bring on the attendant fear.

When the horse left the gate in a gallop, Larry Jennings said, "Now this horse is a legitimate runner. You might say he's finally ready to earn his living. He'll never again approach the gate slowly and never again leave it slowly. He'll know when he leaves the gate he has to leave it in a gallop. When those doors open, he's got to be out of there, and fast. He knows that now. Horses aren't that smart but they're creatures of habit, and it's surprising how quickly they learn. So this two-year-old, when he's brought to the starting gate, why he'll approach it with respect and, yes, a certain amount of fear."

To mitigate the fear Blum brought the horse back to the gate and this time just stood in it with him so that in the future, under actual racing conditions, the horse would not be 100 percent sure that he would have to gallop and compete and, as a consequence, would be less nervous and afraid when confronted with the gate. He would, at least for the better part of his juvenile year, when thoroughbreds were most impressionable and anxious, come to it with mixed emotions.

"Now we got him good and fooled," Larry Jennings said.

A while later Walter Blum was in his car riding to his ocean-front apartment. He was going home earlier than usual this morning because he wanted to get in a longer rest. He was expecting a big afternoon. Still preoccupied, rankled rather, by the subject of holding horses, he said:

"Hell, a jockey's got to be real stupid to hold a horse. Why, when he's performing in a race he's in front of the public first of all, and then he's in front of the stewards. They can see him on the tape. Why they can slow it up, stop it, back it up, reverse, side shot, head shot, front shot, rear shot, man, they can get a shot up your ass.

"If you do something wrong, like I said, they're not stupid. They know what your performance should be like and how you ride and they know when you're doing what you should be doing and when you're not doing what you should be doing.

"Now if you have a bad reputation, they watch you even closer. So the jockey who's going to hold a horse for the sheer purpose of winning a bet, next time he runs, it's not good. It's not good for him. It's not good for his career, for his reputation, or for winning a bet either.

"A lot of times when you give a horse a bum race he doesn't benefit from that race, so the next time he runs and you let him run he might come up short. A horse that gets beat two lengths in a race and is being persevered with, he's benefiting from that race. Next time he runs he's going to be a much sharper horse.

"But a horse that is not being asked for his full ability, well, he's not really extending himself to where he's benefiting from that race for the next time.

"In some cases I've seen jockeys not persevere with their mounts today, and come back next week and persevere with their mounts, thinking they're going to win a bet — and their horse gets beat at the wire, by a head, by a neck, a length or two or three, because the horse got tired.

"Jockey comes back scratching his head saying, 'Shit, this horse got tired.'

"Well, he got tired because he didn't extend himself fully the last time he ran."

Blum now pulled up to the front of his apartment.

"I may be naive," he said. "But I don't think holding horses happens too much today. Today there's too much money to be made by being honest."

Chapter 29

Walter Blum has good reason to be sensitive on the issue of holding horses even though such a charge has never been leveled against him personally. Racing, he says, has been good to him, and he does not like to see its name smeared. It is a fact of life that when one jockey comes under suspicion, the entire profession is held accountable.

He says, "Your everyday racing public thinks there's a lot of shit going on and that there's a lot of cut and dry races. I know for a fact there aren't."

This is essentially true, as far as riders are concerned. But the rider is not the last word. The trainer has plenty to say about a race. More, in fact, than anybody. The trainer, if he so desires, can get his horse beaten very easily without the knowledge of the jockey. For one thing, he can feed his horse on the day of the race. For another, he can instruct his rider to stay off the pace, when he knows the horse is at his best only with the pace. These are the intangible methods.

The more discernible way of influencing the outcome of a race is drugging, an all-too-common practice, especially on the smaller tracks.

In most instances drugs are used on horses for the same reason drugs are used on humans: to ease pain. Yet the drugs that ease pain likewise work as stimulants in some cases and as depressants in others. In fact, the same drug that works as a stimulant on one horse can work as a depressant on another.

The most commonly used drug is Butazolidin, known as Bute, an analgesic. In every state, it is all right to use Bute — and some other analgesics such as aspirin — so long as it does not show up in the post race urinalysis. In some states, indeed, Bute is permitted in horses running in a race, though most states still hold out because Bute often has the effect of a stimulant. Moreover, Bute, and other analgesics, can lull a sore horse into a false sense of security.

This is the area where matters get touchy because trainers are largely within their rights to do all they can to get their horses in running shape, especially when one takes into account the day-to-day pressures, particularly that of meeting the insatiable demands of the Association, which is always appealing for more and more horses to fill cards that seem always to be coming up short. Horses break down, horses get sick, just like humans, and, just like humans, horses need remedies. The trainer has to come up with these remedies or else he is out of business. And as George Towne, the bandleader turned trainer, said, "The biggest pain in the ass the world has ever made is the racehorse."

So the trainer does not have an easy time of it with his horses. He might have twenty horses in his shed row, and each horse is an individual with his own habits, his own requirements. Thus if, on the morning of a day of a race, a horse comes up empty and lifeless, as the result of pain, the trainer might feel he has no choice but to administer a pain killer.

This is the trainers' argument for Bute, and, as arguments go, it's not bad. Not so justifiable, however, is the use of obvious stimulants, such as cocaine, Chromozine, amphetamines, and adrenalin. These are the dangerous drugs. They can kill the horse and get the trainer suspended. Most trainers do not use them. Some do.

Friday Afternoon

Chapter 30

The two races that were of special interest to Pete Mikos this morning were the sixth and the seventh. In the sixth race of the afternoon the trainer Harvey Rosenblatt, a close friend of Pete's, would be represented with Give Me A Story, a horse that would be going off at high odds and could win — had a very good chance of winning — and be the source of food and rent money to those who were on the inside of the information. In the seventh race Harvey Rosenblatt had another horse in with an excellent shot, Mister Market (Walter Blum's Student Lamp aside).

This early in the morning all this was rumor and speculation. The job ahead was to narrow it down to hard truth.

So when the first opportunity — the ten o'clock break — presented itself, Pete Mikos was on his way to the other end of the backstretch and Harvey Rosenblatt's shed row.

Harvey Rosenblatt, who is still in his early twenties, is already a full-fledged, licensed trainer. He is balding in the front and to make up for it, lets his hair grow wild along the sides, sticking out on both sides from under a newspaper boy's cap he always wears. That, along with a sleepy smile and a smooth red complexion, makes him appear even younger than he is. In his first two years he had had a good and a bad start.

First of all he won on the first horse he ever ran. He owned the horse, Bolder 'n Tracy, and it still was in his shed row and still making him money, though now he was more an object of sentimentality than a runner. A few months after Harvey Rosenblatt won his first race on his first try he was at Garden State Racetrack in Cherry Hill, New Jersey, claiming another horse. As was customary and required, Harvey paid out the purchase price, five thousand dollars, in advance, only moments before the claiming race. What he did not do was take out insurance. Most trainers take out insurance when they claim a horse, in case the horse dies in the race. Harvey Rosenblatt did not take out insurance because he was young and reckless, and besides, how often does a horse that is claimed die in the race that he is claimed in, and, what's more, how often does a horse die in a race in the first place?

Not very often. But, of course, the horse did indeed break down and die coming around the turn for home before Harvey Rosenblatt's startled eyes.

The five thousand dollars had not really been Harvey Rosenblatt's. The money belonged to his patron, the prospective owner. When Harvey Rosenblatt later called this man on the phone with the bad news, there was a long pause at the other end of the wire. Then the man said, "Don't let it get you down."

It didn't. Harvey Rosenblatt went on to claim more horses, to make more money. Though his accountant was telling him he was going broke, he was in the money, either win, place, or show, more often than not, more often, in fact, than a trainer of his age had a right to be — about half the time, an incredible percentage.

The truth was Harvey Rosenblatt did not need money. He was rich even before he became a trainer. In fact he was richer before he became a trainer than he was later. His family owned a department store chain in New York. When Harvey Rosenblatt graduated from college and decided to go into training horses, his mother said, "Why can't you be like everybody else and come into the family business?"

Most of the owners Harvey Rosenblatt trained for were friends of the family, rich people who had nothing better to do with their money than spend it on horses and hope for the best — and truly getting the best, for Harvey was producing and making them, if not himself, a profit — a benefit quite uncommon. "They're spoiled rotten," Harvey said.

As a rule, owners were a pain in the neck.

"Take this horse here," Harvey was saying. "He's broken down completely. He used to be a good horse but now he's so sore he can't stand in one place. Poor guy doesn't know what to do with himself. I had the vet over and the vet doesn't know what's wrong with him. So me, I'd like to put him out for a while. About six months, maybe a year. I don't want to run him. The owner doesn't want to hear that. The owner wants him to run. That's the kind of people you got to deal with."

The horse's tendons were inflamed, and he was running a fever. This much you could tell by just putting your hand to his joints. On a healthy horse the limbs are ice cold. On a sick horse, such as this one, the limbs are hot. There is hardly a sadder sight than a sick horse.

When Pete Mikos came by, Harvey was preparing the whirlpool bath for his sick horse to get his blood circulating again. The other seven horses under Harvey's care were meanwhile being cooled by huge fans; each stall, each horse, had its own individual fan, the blades going round and round. "Horses are like people," Harvey said. "They get hot, too." Most trainers, in order to save on electricity, did not use fans on all their horses in the summer. It was this kind of extra effort on the part of Harvey Rosenblatt that made him the superb trainer that he was. "In a couple of years Harvey's going to be the greatest trainer in the country," Pete Mikos said.

Pete Mikos himself would one day make a great trainer. What he did not have presently were Harvey's resources. What he already had in abundance was knowledge and love of horses. This was best illustrated some weeks before when Danny Perlsweig left him in charge of the shed row for the few days he would be at Saratoga buying yearlings. Pete had orders to enter a certain horse in the race of a certain day. When the day came the horse, in Pete's opinion, was in no shape to do any running. He had bucked shins (cannon bone inflammation). He needed rest. So Pete scratched him and later called Danny Perlsweig in Saratoga, telling him what he had done, or rather not done. Danny was not especially pleased. The next race the horse was in he won.

Mister Market, the three-year-old Harvey Rosenblatt had in the seventh race, was in his stall neighing.

"Gonna have to geld that horse," Harvey said. "Look at him every time that filly walks by. He goes crazy. Goes out of his mind. He's got nothing on his mind but broads." Every time the filly walked by — as she was being hotwalked around the shed row — Mister Market neighed, kicked, and threw his head around. Harvey said this preoccupation with girl horses was keeping Mister Market from concentrating on his job, namely, racing. Still, he should run well today. He should give Walter Blum's Student Lamp a run for the money. "If he can get his mind off the broads," Harvey said.

A few stalls down from Mister Market was Give Me A Story, Harvey's hope in the sixth. Give Me A Story was not so crazy about girls. He was a gelding, and he was in a mean, hostile mood. He bared his teeth and tried to take a bite out of Pete Mikos' hand when Pete went to massage his face. "Mean son of a bitch," Pete said, laughing.

"Yeah, he's nice and mean," Harvey said, full of pride. "He's gonna run good today. He's gonna run real good. He runs good when he's mean."

Here was where the trainer and his confidants had it over everybody else. Nobody else knew that this horse was, this morning, as fit as could be, as fit and on the muscle as he hadn't been in months. The paper showed that in the last few months he had run very poorly. So it figured he would run poorly again and therefore go off at very high odds. Unknown to the public was the fact that Give Me A Story had sizzled in a work the other day. Yes, the time was properly recorded in the paper; what was not recorded was the fact that the horse had been extremely willing and, in the days that followed the workout, had become impatient with the routine that required him to remain in his stall twenty-three hours a day. He was pent up and full of desire, and this manifested itself in anger. A thousand pound mass of energy, he was a most satisfying sight to his trainer.

Another indication that the horse was in peak form was his appetite. In recent mornings he had taken to his feed vigorously, eating all that was put before him and more — including the stall door, at which he chewed away like a woodpecker.

This assured sense of being is the beauty of a racer. The mystery, too. There are times when he is hollow and dead inside, like a man in the mid stages of a hangover. The emptiness shows in his eyes, in his manners, and, paramountly, in his appetite — he does not eat. Brought to the track for a race or a workout, he is manifestly uninterested. His action is sluggish and loose. The rider can sense this right away. This horse, he knows, is dead. Nothing. Empty. Going through the motions and that's all. Back in his stall the horse stands back feebly, not bothering to stick his head out the top opening.

What made him one way or the other was the mystery that tantalized every trainer.

There are horses who are simply above it all. They approach the gate with lofty disdain. Such a horse was Jaikyl, a stunning, majestic gray once trained by Danny Perlsweig. After having won a number of important stakes, one day he apparently decided he had had enough of racing. From then on he was virtually impossible to get to the gate. Once in the gate, and out of the gate, he let the other horses break and gallop. He himself just stood his ground as if thinking, "What the hell is all this going to prove?" In the end he was put out to pasture. He was said to be a "smart" horse, smart like a nine-to-fiver who one day decides not to punch his time-card.

But to go back to Give Me A Story: when Harvey Rosenblatt has a horse he is sure of, as he was sure of Give Me A Story, he is not moved to shout the news from the nearest rooftop. Nor is he compelled to run along the streets tearing his clothes for joy, yelling out the information to the passers-by. What he does is keep the information to himself, largely, and when, on occasion, he is disposed to share it, he shares it with a friend or two — by covert means. That is to say he does not tell a friend, "Hey, have I got a horse for you!" Rather, in response to an inquiry, he smiles. To the perceptive inquisitor that would be answer enough.

So having already told Pete Mikos that Give Me A Story would run well, the tag — *how* well — was revealed in a smile.

Pete, for his part, was just as subtle. His method of extracting the information had been simply to appear.

To the backstretch insider wagering is an endeavor more private than sex. For a groom (or anybody else of secondary rank) it is more embarrassing to be caught placing a bet than it is to be caught with a hand in somebody's pants, because only fools had the audacity, born out of naivete, to favor one horse over another. Racing is a game that turns the tables on you every time. Wagering is an enterprise limited to the frivolous few.

The knowledgeable insider is expected to be cynical, wise from his special perspective, hardened by what he knows. And he knows, above everything else, that nothing is certain. The sure bet, the superior horse of the field, can stumble in the gate or, equally plausible, be under a rider who is holding him. Or anything.

Still and all, one has to eat. And on his wages alone the groom (or the assistant trainer) cannot eat well. He works hard enough. He is at his shed row by five or six in the morning (seven days a week) mucking out the stalls, then resupplying the stalls with fresh hay, soon after mixing the feed (vitamins included) in the feed bins, then feeding the horses, then hosing the horses, then bandaging the horses, and when all that, and more, is done, his afternoons are spent in the shed row keeping watch over the horses that are to race that afternoon — to see that they are not tampered with by outsiders, opposing trainers, or a groom with a grudge and a score to settle.

Then, too, his life is always in danger. There is no telling what a horse will do in his stall, the groom in there with him. When the horse rears and kicks, the groom, confined in the same nine by twelve quarters, cannot always get out of the way in time and, likewise, cannot always withdraw an accessible face, behind, or arm fast enough when the horse is in a mood to bite.

For all this, he is paid from seventy to one hundred and twenty dollars a week. Of course he is always complaining. According to one groom, a veteran of many a backside, "You won't find justice in this game. Like the jockey's on the horse one minute and he gets paid a thousand bucks. The groom's with the horse all day and he gets paid peanuts.

"Risk? Compared to the groom, the jockey don't know from risk. The groom's life is ten times more in danger than the jockey's. Me, when it comes around to risk, I'll change places with a rider any day.

"Okay, so you got this difference with the rider. What's worse is your relationship with the trainer. There are exceptions, but from what I know most trainers don't give a hoot's ass about their grooms. Like if they know something about their horse, the last person they're gonna tell is the groom. I mean if the trainer knows his horse is a winner, he sure ain't gonna tell the groom. 'Cause he wants to keep his groom under his foot. He don't want him making any money. He wants him poor. He wants him down. He's afraid if the groom makes some money he'll bug out and leave him. So he don't give him no information and he pays him dirt and he treats him like dirt."

So to compensate, grooms and others on the periphery are on the constant prowl for the good information, the bread-winning horse.

As Pete and Harvey stood talking — Harvey now holding by the shank a horse grazing in the meadow in front of his shed row — one perceived in them an incomparable sense of pleasure in being young and alive. In Pete especially there was the pure, ingenuous delight of being alive and of knowing that all that was good was yet to come. He had the abandon and the free ways of a cavalier. He was a young man pleased with himself and certain of what he did. Unlike most men in their early twenties he was not tortured by the demons of doubt or debilitated by the larger questions of survival.

That nonsense they teach you in college. Along the backstretch they teach you clarity and singleness of purpose; those who learn survive and ask no questions as to the meaning of it all. A stable full of solid horses is meaning enough. Along the backstretch the riddle of life is resolved in the next race. Philosophy is the study of what form a race will take. Existentialism is the acceptance that the other man's horse is better than yours.

In this world Pete Mikos functioned and thrived, for he had plans. Some day he would go off to Europe — France, England, where it had all begun and where they still ran their races backwards, clockwise — and expand his purview, learn the classics of horsemanship from the masters. Meanwhile, he would learn all he could from an American master, Danny Perlsweig, who though lacking in finesse, somehow always managed to work his horses into top condition, actually sharpening them into condition by racing them over and over again, so that he was usually most indomitable in the waning days of a meet.

There were others to learn from too, many of them, the good ones, right here at Monmouth no farther than a shed row away — among them the ex-pharmaceutics salesman, Lou Goldfine, who would propose that a trainer in the midst of a slump take the cue from baseball and bench himself (and his entire shed row) until he felt himself ready again, using this time, perhaps, to ponder the wisdom of conditioning a great horse such as his own Shecky Greene (Raggedy Ann). Whenever Raggedy's groom approached him with the flat statement, "There's something I want you to know about Raggedy," Goldfine would, he would say, "have heart failure." And then there was the seasoned John Kulina, a truly fine trainer, who once advised against the hiring of girls as stablehands because "they do nothing but get you into trouble and distract the boys from their work." "Once," he cited, "I went against my better judgment and hired a girl. A college girl. Nice girl. Nice college girl. One morning I find this nice college girl in the tack room having a go at it with this nothing of a groom. A real loser. I asked this girl, I took her aside later and I asked her, 'What's the future in this?' "

Pete Mikos would listen to all these stories and laugh at the funny ones and remember the serious ones for the day he would be on his own. (In his words: "On the backstretch every man has his story. Every man is a man on his way up or a man on his way down. You learn from everybody.") Then one day on his own — next year, the year after, whenever — he would, he was determined, be an honest trainer, like Harvey Rosenblatt, and take no shortcuts. He would have consideration for his horses and show them the kindess they deserved.

For the time being he was working hard but enjoying himself. And what greater joy than having a good thing in the sixth!

Chapter 31

Harvey Rosenblatt was going with the irrepressible Miguel Rivera on Give Me A Story in the sixth race. Rivera, Lovato, and Kevin Daly were the riders he used most frequently. He liked them not because they were capable but because, in his mind, they evinced kindness for their mounts, a quality, he felt, that was lacking in most riders, among them Walter Blum.

"Walter Blum has no respect for the horses he rides," Harvey said as he walked Give Me A Story along the backstretch horse path on the way to the paddock. "He rides them for his own good. Doesn't give a damn what happens to the horse. I used him once. After the race, when I asked him what happened, he just walked away. Well, the horse can't tell you what happened and the only way you're going to know how to condition him after a race is by what the jockey tells you. A rider that cares about horses is going to tell you, 'Look, this horse ran a bit sore.' Okay, so you go from there. But if a rider won't tell you, well, it makes it all the harder for you. I guess Blum's too big to talk to trainers anymore."

So there it is. Not everybody loves Walter Blum. Still, for each trainer who finds fault with him there are nine who think him the greatest. The last thing they would say is that he is inconsiderate to them and unkind, unfeeling, to their horses.

In fact, at times he seems to go overboard in his desire to please trainers, as for example, when, early in the morning, he makes the rounds of the shed rows (something he did not have to do this meet), positively solicitous in his inquiries, and, later, in the afternoon, after a race, explaining his performance quarter pole to quarter pole.

Still, there are trainers he will never please, and in the case of Harvey Rosenblatt, there is the friction that attends the joining of seasoned pro and tenderfoot to one cause. The backside, after all, secluded and separate world that it is, also has its generation gap wherein the under-30s, to which group Harvey Rosenblatt certainly belongs, mistrust (charitable phrase) their elders — the Establishment, of which Walter Blum certainly is a part.

That Walter Blum cares deeply for his horses is irrefutable. So it is a question of degrees. He did not, apparently, from Harvey Rosenblatt's view, care for them enough — enough to please him, and being of the new generation, he was a hard man to please.

Leading up to the sixth race Walter Blum had had an indifferent, quiet afternoon — still, of course, one short of his 4,000. In the first race he came in next to last on Lucky Caper, who was sent off the favorite. She went off the favorite just because she had Walter Blum on her and almost everybody was certain that with Walter Blum wanting his 4,000th win so badly he would, if he had to, carry the horse across the finish line, which was exactly what he would have had to do to get anywhere with this horse.

Then, too, 4,000 aside, Walter Blum is of the caliber that is always bet down. His agent, Dave Hart, is quick to recognize this. "He rides a lot of horses that are false favorites," he said shortly after Blum rode out this one.

Blum did not contest the second, third, fourth, and fifth races. He sat them out at poolside.

He was to ride Compatriot in the sixth.

Walter Blum, however, was not the only thing that was happening this fine afternoon. In the first race, for example, Paul Kallai provided a memorable moment for a Hungarian woman in a big straw hat who was at the racetrack for the first time in her life and, being unlearned in the arcane language of the *Daily Racing Form*, employed the unsophisticated but often profitable method of handicapping the jockeys rather than the horses. "Kallai," she said, moments before the race, "must be Hungarian."

When the ten horses came onto the main track for the pre-race parade, she stood on her toes and yelled out something in Hungarian. The startled Kallai reflexively turned his head in her direction and winked. Well, besides being the "biggest thrill" of her life, it gave her all the incentive she needed, and she hurriedly placed a two dollar bet on Kallai's Iron Ruler Lady, who went off at 14 to 1 and later, when she came in first, paid a hefty thirty dollars. "Ah, Budapest, my Budapest," said the transported woman.

Carlos Barrera won the second race on Cheers Nation after Craig Perret's Hi Way Bowl had led most of the way. Craig Perret was Lou Goldfine's and Shecky Greene's regular rider and thus a rider of some renown. Perret has a kindly manner and handles himself well; despite his youth and success, he is easy to talk to and quick to express his delight at having such good fortune come his way in Shecky Greene — the superb horse being as much a fluke to the rider as he was to the trainer. At that point Shecky Greene still had never been headed in a sprint and had recently broken two track records in Florida.

Sam Manzi, Perret's agent, was observing his boy's performance on Hi Way Bowl, watching the race from the television in the clubhouse by the tunnel. After the race, Sam Manzi said, "I'm getting better every day." Agents frequently spoke of their clients in the first person singular; if a rider had a headache, his agent often took aspirins. "I'm getting better and better. Okay, you can't tell that too much on this race, which is just another race on just another horse. Although, yeah, with a little bit of luck I could have won this one — but my horse got tired. But I win my share. You watch me day in day out and there's no question I'm getting to be the best. I'll tell you how you can tell if a rider's any good. A rider that's any good you watch him what he does when he come from behind. When he starts making his move. The good rider, he does everything smooth, all in one motion. Like my boy, he don't lunge forward. I used to. I used to jerk my horses. Now I do it real smooth. The horse don't even know he's being asked.

"That's the way Howard Grant rides 'em, and I used to handle Grant's book. Grant's got all these personal problems, you know, weight, but he's still the greatest rider there is. The greatest white rider. I mean now you got all these Latins and they've just about taken over. Most of the good ones are the Latins anymore. But Grant is still the greatest. Nobody come off the pace like Howard Grant. Why I seen him on horses I thought were dead beat and coming around the turn for home, I don't know what he does, but he does something, and he win.

"Right after Grant I'd have to pick Baeza — he's a picture on a horse — then Vasquez, then Pincay, then Cordero, then Velasquez, and my boy next."

What about Blum, Hole, Bracciale? "Blum? He's all right. But he's rich now. He's got all the money he needs, so he don't have to take no chances and he don't take 'em. Hole? He's nothing but an average rider. I'll say this: He works hard on a horse, he's always working, and he's an honest rider. Bracciale? Come on! What the hell, everybody knows he's trying to imitate Howard Grant's style. He's nowhere near a Howard Grant. Never gonna be. Yeah he gets a lot of winners but what about the winners he don't get? He gets more mounts than anybody and there's a lot of races he should win that he don't. He's just lucky he got a good agent. Real, hardworking agent. To me, Bracciale ain't much. My boy is ten times better than him. Right now, right here, I'd say Craig Perret is the best. Don't just ask me. Ask anybody."

Which, when you did, yielded conflicting results, as every agent thought his boy to be the best — "Ask anybody."

Steve Neff won the third race on Poncho Mesa but the focus of interest, to some at least, was John Mallano, the former hot apprentice of New York who had finally got a mount — Strawberry Royale, whom he brought in a nice close second, displaying, to those who had followed him in New York, "the form of old." Later in the jockeys' room Mallano flashed a rare smile and said, "Maybe this is gonna be my new start."

To get a true picture of a race, you do not so much have to watch the race as watch the trainer who has a competitive horse in the running — like Herb Paley, in the fourth. Between the time his horse, Friendsville, broke from the gate to the time he crossed the finish line a minute and eleven seconds later, Herb Paley was a man going through the anguish of a deeply personal hell. If the agent is one with the rider, so much more the trainer, who is one with the rider and the horse. He can truly say "I" when speaking of the rider and think of the horse as an extension of himself — or, during an actual race, be an extension of the horse. No, actually *be* the horse.

Almost everything that makes up the horse comes from the trainer. Even the animal's comportment can, in many cases, be traced to the trainer. Ron Gibson, the dry-humored, rough-and-tumble trainer from Montreal, Canada, liked to say, "You can usually tell by looking in a man's shed row how successful he is. If it's clean, he's probably a successful trainer." Miserable surroundings make for a miserable horse. A clean, happy shed row generally makes for a contented horse just as a clean, happy home generally makes for a contented child, and, to stretch the metaphor, the trainer takes as much pride in his horse's performance as a parent a child's. For this reason it is often very painful for a trainer to have his horse claimed. The trainer Joe Yannuzzi tells the story of entering his favorite horse in a claimer obviously below his level, to win a bet during hard times, and the hurt of walking back to the shed row after the race without the horse.

In the running of the fourth race, one could perceive in Herb Paley's transparent face the travails of Friendsville and Michael Hole, Friendsville's rider. When they were in the gate, Herb Paley held his breath — much as horses did. Some horses do not resume breathing until three or four strides away from the gate; some not until halfway through the race, at which point they are out of breath and out of the running (these horses were known as horses with "cheap speed," but for the wrong reasons). Many persons believe that a racer is at the mercy of his anatomy, and though that is true to some measure, he is more liable to his breath control than to anything else. The breathing, actually, is the governing factor in the racer. The gifted horse saves his breath but does not hold it; the poor horse holds it until he can hold it no longer. Here, too, in the breathing, one finds the key that differentiates the router from the sprinter. The router is the smaller horse, the horse in whom the oxygen circulates fully and rapidly. The router also is the horse that instinctively paces — rates — his breathing. So actually, when one speaks of a horse rating himself, one really speaks of his breathing.

When Friendsville and Michael Hole were away from the gate, Herb Paley shared with them the agony of a slow start. His face was in a full grimace, his fists were tightly clenched, and, as though trying to do the horse's running, he shuffled his feet and rocked his body back and forth. As if receiving the message, the horse responded by smoothing his rhythm and elongating his stride. When Friendsville was still behind but joining the leaders, Herb Paley rocked back and forth, faster and faster, in time to the horse's rhythm. Coming around the three-eighth pole, horse, rider, and trainer were one as they passed one runner, then another, then another, then another. Approaching the turn for home, the unit of three took in a deep breath of air, held it to the quarter pole, and let it out in a powerful gust on the turn. Along the stretch, with one horse to overtake, Herb Paley demanded more speed and to convey this thought rocked his body and jutted his head a beat faster than the horse. Again yielding to the celestial voice, the horse let go with a rampageous expulsion of speed, exchanging extension and retraction of foot with such rapidity that he was almost flying (the fractions, 21 4/5, :45, 1:11 attested to that), and, with his faculties extended to the fullest, his rhythm now one with his trainer's, together they huffed and pumped their way past the one obstructive horse and crossed the finish line and bore the elation of coming in first — later, seconds later, to grow limp, droopy, and lightheaded in a haze of spent passion and anticlimax.

Herb Paley's fists now came undone, his face muscles slackened, and he even smiled.

Chapter 32

Though Pete Mikos was not subject to philosophical meanderings, he did have his codes. The one he lived by was this: "You take your shot and hope for the best." Furthermore, if your shot missed or backfired, no big deal. You went on. Did not look back. This approach saw him through the small things, like betting, and the big things, like banking on the assumption that someday he would become a trainer. The most important by-product of his code was impassivity: stoicism. What you never did was show emotion, or even involvement. When they saw you involved, interested, or concerned in something, they watched you, and if you lost, they would privately or publicly make fun of you. When you lost, something rancid in you was revealed. You became ugly. When you won, it was good and manly to show you cared, had cared all along. When you lost, it was embarrassing. So you kept your plans and hopes to yourself.

Guided by this principle, Pete Mikos would be damned if he would let anybody know that he was putting a few dollars on Give Me A Story. When the horses for the sixth race finished parading before the grandstand and the clubhouse, the odds on Give Me A

Story were 19 to 1, and Pete Mikos said, "I'm going to get me a hot dog."

While Pete Mikos went to get his hot dog or whatever, Humberto Gracia drank a glass of beer in the terrace of the clubhouse. The sun was beating down hard and he was sitting at a table that was shaded by an overhead umbrella. Except for a straggler here and there and a few girls from the publicity office, there was nobody else on or around the terrace. Almost everybody was in the building making his bet, or out front already. Some of the girls from the publicity office were sitting on the lounge chairs immediately below the terrace sunning themselves, and one of them, Linda Rasmussen, Monmouth Park's beautiful official greeter, was talking with Paul DeMarco, Mickey Solomone's agent, who was being flirtatious. Mickey Solomone, who was standing on the porch of the administration building, also was talking to a girl.

Humberto Gracia saw none of this. He was having his beer facing a wall. He did not want to be seen drinking a beer. There is nothing wrong with having a beer, but if a trainer or an owner saw you having one, he might jump to conclusions. Humberto Gracia averaged no more than one or two glasses of beer a day and he drank them only when it was very hot, when he was very drained, and when he had no more mounts to ride — all of which was the case at this point of the afternoon. He had had a nothing of an afternoon. He had been on only one mount, Best Amber, in the fifth, and had come in seventh in a field of eight. He had no further mounts the rest of the afternoon.

He said: "You take the good with the bad, no?"

He thought about that for a while and then said, "Tomorrow I think I will have a better day. Today I think is Blum's day. Everybody has his time, his day. It is this way in everything. In racing it is even more the truth." He smiled for emphasis. His teeth glistened. His teeth were so shiny you could comb your hair by them.

"The most important thing for a rider," he said, "is to never get down. Never get low. So low that you can never get up — and there are riders who get that low. You must wait. Be patient. It will come. I have times when it is easy to be low, but I stay up. I tell myself it will get better, and it does. For example, one day you have no mounts, the next day you have mounts but you have no winners, and the third day you have many mounts and many winners. That is the way it is."

Humberto Gracia was still the talented Latin who had not made it big — big like, say, Jacinto Vasquez or Jorge Velasquez, to name those of his age. He was their equal in talent but had had that immigration problem and, anyway, for whatever reason, did not carry the majestic aura that attended Vasquez and Velasquez (and of course Baeza). When he walked into the jocks' room, he was still just another jock — a good, hard working jock, but nothing too special. Vasquez had been at Monmouth a few days earlier, for the day (he was riding at Saratoga), and the lift he gave the jocks' room was something remarkable to see. Monmouth had its own holy men, Blum and Bracciale, but Vasquez was a prophet from another land. He departed with this message: "A rider will never show his class on a bad horse."

This then (assuming you had class) was the secret — and to Humberto Gracia, the problem. So far no Executioners (Vasquez), no Desert Vixens (Velasquez), and no Linda's Chief had come his way to boost him to prominence and make his name well known among trainers and owners. So he was the one very talented Latin still struggling, and consequently recognition, when it came, as it would, would be all the more sweet. Humberto Gracia would one day be called a great rider.

He was on his second beer when Pete Mikos came over. Pete was happy and nervous about something. He had that kind of a smile. He was also impatient about something. He asked Humberto how he was, how he was doing, and then invited him to a party. Pete shared an apartment with three grooms, and the four of them were throwing a party later on that night. Humberto smiled and bowed in the courtly style of the old world, said he was grateful for the invitation but could not attend. He had sleep to catch up on. He had an apartment by the ocean and was kept up practically every night by people having parties. Pete laughed and then said he was going out front to watch the race.

Crossing over from the clubhouse to the grandstand Pete gave the guard a cold stare. Moving away from him, Pete said, "These guards are a pain in the ass. A few days ago I tried to get from the grandstand to the clubhouse and this guard here says, 'Let's see your pass.' Shit, that guy knows I work here. He sees me every day. He just likes to throw his weight around. They all do. Now if I was dressed up in a sharp suit and everything, they wouldn't be bugging me every time. They know they couldn't get away with that shit with the big shots, so they pick on the lower echelons. Hell, if you'd let them they'd step all over you. You got to watch out for yourself."

This echoed the view once expressed by Pete Fantini who, though a novice, had learned quickly enough that in the daily life of the racetrack "it's every man for himself." It also pointed to the intensity of the many small wars that rage three-quarters below the surface on all corners of the front- and backside. There are the trainers who try to get out from under the owners, the jockeys who try to get out from under the trainers, and the grooms who try to get out from under everybody. The grooms probably have it the worst, but the riders do not have it so good, either. Jockeys are answerable to practically all comers, to the racing commission, to the stewards, to the owners, to the trainers, to their fellow jockeys, and, of course, to the bettors. Yet it is the clerk of scales who can make life most miserable for a jockey. If he has it *in* for a certain rider, he can make an issue over those extra few ounces — that additional weight that is usually disregarded and goes unreported — and set him down. He can also (through the stewards) fine the rider if he reports in late in the morning or the afternoon. Late can be three minutes. These things do not happen often, but they do happen and they serve to remind the rider that with all the glory, he is still a subject. A working stiff.

Still, someone like Pete Mikos can always say that the rider at least gets *paid* for all his trouble.

The horses for the sixth race were now approaching the starting gate. Pete Mikos stood in front of the rail of the grandstand, near the tunnel and the finish line. Next to him was Harvey Rosenblatt, adjusting his binoculars. He trained his binoculars on Give Me A Story, as did the grooms and hotwalkers who were friends of Pete and Harvey. They all had bets on Give Me A Story. Some had bet their week's wages on him. There had been fear that word of the hot tip would get around, but it hadn't. Give Me A Story was going off at 19 to 1. In fact he was the longest shot of the field.

Blum and Compatriot were going off at four to one. The favorite was B. B. Martin, ridden by Carlos Barrera and trained by Ron Gibson, who happened to be standing a few feet away from Pete and Harvey and who had just had his B. B. Martin claimed from him. Ron Gibson was puffing nervously on his cigarette. Ron Gibson was a tough, nervous little guy from the west side of Montreal. He had done most of his hanging around on the street corners of downtown Montreal with other tough, nervous little guys — gansters, he would say, half jokingly. He was now in his early forties and upset at having had a good horse claimed from him. "This is a cutthroat business," he said, watching the horses come within a few minutes of the gate. "Sure you claim horses. I claim horses, everybody claims horses. Only sometimes it surprises you who does the claiming. Sometimes your best fucking friend will claim a horse off you. You think you had an understanding with him, you know, kind of an unwritten, unmentioned understanding, and the next thing you know he's got a claim in for your horse. That's the way this fucking game is.

"Yeah, you can always claim the horse back, but then he's in jail and anyway, I don't like to claim a horse back. Never works out. Horse never runs the same for you again. That's one of the strange things about this business. Anyway, what the fuck. I mean there's no friendship in this racket. The guy in the next shed row, the guy you had coffee with earlier in the morning, he's the guy that might claim your horse. So what the fuck. You just can't give a shit. This much is sure: You got to really love this business to be in it. I love it all right, but some of the people . . . I mean, you walk around the backside and see what happens when you ask somebody what they think about what's going on in Chile. Nine times out of ten you know what they'll tell you? 'Chili? Don't care for the stuff. Burns my tongue.' That's right. That's the kind of people you deal with every day.

"Nothing new to me of course. I've been hanging around with the worst kinds of people all my life. You have your better class too, sure, but even they can be low. For example, this one owner owned near a quarter of all my horses. I made the guy twenty-two thousand bucks last month. Now that's doing good. Real good. So what the fuck's he doing? He's pulling out all his horses. Going into training himself. I made it look easy for the son of a bitch. So there you are. And now I got this horse I just lost to a claim." He brought the binoculars to his eyes and said, "Submarine you every time."

Farther to the right of Pete Mikos was Jim Raftery. He was in the winner's circle with the "4,000" sign set before him. Jane Goldstein and some of the other publicity people were in the winner's circle, too, and for a few seconds it looked like they had the right idea.

Compatriot (Blum), Rosaryville (Hole), and Zoom Loom (Cusimano) were the early pace setters in this mile and a sixteenth contest, and Blum especially seemed well spotted, laying second. For the better part of the race it was these three and these three only: Zoom Loom on the lead, Rosaryville third, close enough to take over at any time, and Compatriot in between, always within striking distance. The rest of the field was conducting another business. Straightening out for home, Blum and Hole went to the whip as each made his bid to overtake the leader, Zoom Loom, who was tiring. For a moment — when he closed the gap to a length — Blum looked like he might have it, but then his horse tired, too, and Hole, it was now plain, was on a horse that had given all he had in the chase and had no more to give. Now, though still traveling at some thirty miles an hour, the three leaders seemed to be standing still, as though just waiting to be gobbled up, and when the rest of the field, still fresh and full of run, closed in the three appeared to be running backward — it was almost comical. Coming on the strongest were Vincent Bracciale, Jr., on Blazing Tropics and Miguel Rivera's Give Me A Story.

Give Me A Story was the first of the two to make a big move. For an instant he had the lead to himself, but it was still too early for Harvey Rosenblatt, Pete Mikos, and their friends to celebrate for Bracciale, whose Blazing Tropics had at one stage been twelve lengths behind, was gaining on Give Me A Story with every stride.

In the last panel the two hooked up side to side, going for the wire neck to neck, nose to nose.

For the most part the race had gone as planned by Harvey Rosenblatt, who had expected the front-runners to burn out and had instructed his rider, Rivera, to stay off the pace, to come on with a big consuming rush at the end. Only he had not counted on being threatened by a horse and rider following the exact same game plan. No trouble was expected, at least not from Blazing Tropics.

So when it got down to the wire it was a race between the hot horse and the hot rider. And when Blazing Tropics edged out in front of Give Me A Story by a head at the start of the final half panel, Harvey Rosenblatt went limp, Pete Mikos shook his head, and the others around them, those who had backed Give Me A Story with their hard-earned money, reacted in similar displeasure, conceding that when a rider was hot, it was not wise to bet against him.

For Harvey Rosenblatt, as for most trainers, the second guessing began even before the race was over. Why had the rider waited that long to make his move? Or should he have waited even longer? Was it maybe the horse? Was the horse not fit enough? If so, what had he, the trainer, done wrong in the conditioning?

These were the questions Harvey Rosenblatt was asking himself when his horse fell back by a head. Some questions, of course, are beyond answers — like the question of what quality in the horse gives him "heart," the desire to win. There are horses, for example, that simply refuse to let other horses get in front of them — Secretariat and Mr. Correlation, when he is right, come immediately to mind in this category. Then there are horses that have every quality but desire, that feel most comfortable when behind another horse and will not pass the front horse even if the front horse extends a formal invitation. Then again there are horses that will run only when challenged, their specialty being to play catch-up; often this type of runner, if he happens to get out front, will wait for the others to catch up to him before getting serious.

Heart, or courage, generally are not something a trainer can feed a horse. The horse has to have it in himself. There are exceptions. There are horses in whom the courage can be brought out, as was the case of Riva Ridge. At the outset of his career he would fall back and give up as soon as a competitor drew up to him. Then his rider, Ron Turcotte, came up with the idea of putting blinkers on him so that he would not know that he was being challenged, and after a while he got so used to winning that he became practically unbeatable even without blinkers.

And now as Blazing Tropics and Give Me A Story forged to the wire as a unit all that stood between them was desire. The race, as happened with most races this close, would go to the horse that wanted it most. On this day that happened to be Give Me A Story, who regained the lost distance by practically throwing himself at the wire, finishing in front of Blazing Tropics by a head.

The group around Pete Mikos and Harvey Rosenblatt was ecstatic. "Made the rent money," one groom said.

A wide, uncontrollable grin crossed Pete Mikos's face. "Nice," he said.

Chapter 33

Walter Blum sat in front of his locker breathing very heavily, the dust and dirt of the race still on him, all over his face, his body, his silks. The dust on his face made his face gray. When it rained out there and the track was muddy, his face was black. Today it was gray. Walter Blum rubbed his eyes. Some jockeys used Murine for their eyes; Walter Blum rubbed them. Had he been out front all the way his face would not have been as dusty and dirty. As it was, he was not out front all the way; in fact, he came in second to last. So he suffered the indignity of having one horse after another kick dust into his face and eyes. There were many reasons for winning, for wanting to win, and not the least important of them was to be in a position where other horses could not kick dust and mud into your face and eyes. When you were ahead, in front of the others, you got to kick dust and mud into *their* faces and eyes. (Somewhere in this was a deeper message.)

Walter Blum was hunched over on the chair that faced his locker. He licked his lips, gulping frequently. But he could not summon saliva. He was dry inside and out. He was wrung out like a rag and in about fifteen minutes he would have to be out there again fresh and strong. His body would have to regain its vitality without external stimulants, like food. It would have to rebound through the will of the mind. Strength and weakness were psychological. Strength came out of weakness through sheer willpower. At least that's what Walter Blum believed, and it had to have some truth in it for the process of *thinking* a body back to strength worked well for him. There was no question that sitting on a horse in a race — that is, sitting and pulling and yanking and steering a thousand pound animal — took all the strength out of you even though it all lasted hardly more than a minute. But it was equally true that strength could be restored through will.

When Walter Blum regained his breath, began breathing evenly again, he stripped to his pants and flailed his arms as though trying to shake off the kinks of the muscles, which were drum tight. Then he slipped out of his white, now gray, pants, wrapped himself around in a towel, and walked to the shower room, passing a few jockeys who were already getting dressed for the next race and a few who were still coming down off the previous race, one still heaving from the dryness.

In the shower room Walter Blum asked the masseur, Nick Pompilio, where the ice bucket was. Nick Pompilio, who was massaging Phil Grimm, said the ice bucket was where it always was. Walter Blum told Nick Pompilio to go fuck himself. Nick Pompilio, feigning anger, had a similar suggestion for Walter Blum. Phil Grimm laughed.

Walter Blum took a cube of ice out of the ice bucket and brought it to his lips and smeared his lips with it and said, "Ahhhh," as though he had just finished a sumptuous meal. He then removed the towel from around his waist and slapped it, gently, on Nick Pompilio's back. Then before Nick Pompilio could catch him, he was in the shower under a stream of warm water. Nick Pompilio, digging his fingers into Phil Grimm's flesh once again, laughed and said, "That guy, I swear."

Back in front of his locker within five minutes, Walter Blum got dressed in his new silks — his valet had laid them out for him — his energy, his vitality, obviously returned to him. He was feeling good and optimistic and looking forward to the next race. That the next race could bring him his 4,000th win was important to him, but, equally, coming to his fortieth year and twentieth year as a rider he still experienced the same enthusiasm for a race as he had twenty years ago — well, almost.

There were times, he said, when he did not much care for the job of riding. But then there were times, like today, when there was nothing to beat it. Especially satisfying was the continual prospect of victory. A rider came up against his peers every day and was tested and measured against them, and there was deep pleasure in that, in the combat itself, and the knowledge that victory, redemption, was always no more than a half hour away from defeat. Few men had that opportunity — the opportunity to test themselves and measure themselves against their peers and that, obviously, led to frustration, a frustration totally alien to the athlete, especially the jockey, who lived on competition, in its purest sense, and fed his soul on revenge. There was, to be sure, frustration for the jockey, and that came when he knew that he did not measure up. But even then, when he did not measure up, there was no vagueness about it. Except for a few borderline cases it was always easy to tell bad from good.

For Walter Blum there had been some twenty years of success, and yet each day had its own requirement and each race was another test. Like the veteran comedian whose entire career is judged on his latest performance or the venerable author who is judged on his last book, the journeyman jockey is judged on his last race. If he fails in it, there is that much more pressure on him for the next race, and if he loses that and then another he faces a confidence crisis and meets up with a challenge even more treacherous than that of confronting his peers — that of confronting himself. The rider can one day start a tailspin into an abyss from which he never returns, and there is no telling on what day it will happen, if at all, how it will happen, or why it will happen. (For Walter Blum it started immediately after he won his 4,000th race. For some unexplainable reason he went for weeks without a win — though eventually he came out of it.) That, knowing that one day you would win your last race, plus the more obvious fear of being carried off the track on a stretcher, weighs heavily on a jockey's mind before a race. Walter Blum once stated the case rather simply: "You can get killed and that'll be it." In Walter Blum the fear is revealed in long stretches of silence, in sentences suddenly cut short, in warmth abruptly turned to frigidity. And now, confident as he was of winning the next race, his 4,000th, he could not be unaware of the irony of his situation, if only subconsciously. He had, after all, been seriously injured, nearly killed, on the very last day of a year in which he won the nation's riding championship. Fate had a way of giving and taking, of giving one thing and taking another, of evening things out.

Buttoning up his silks, Walter Blum was silent and meditative, thinking his thoughts, and not responding to the jokes coming his way from the riders around him who were not riding in the upcoming race. The pressures were on him, and he had to sort them out. He smoked a cigarette.

Moments later, dressed grandly in his silks of pink and blue, white pants, blue cap, black boots, his arms folded behind him and the whip dangling in the back, a half smile playing on his face, his left eyebrow arched, he stood in the doorway of the jockeys' room looking out at the crowd gathered along the paddock fence, the picture of arrogance.

Harvey Rosenblatt's Mister Market, Frank Lovato up, menaced the leader, Student Lamp, Walter Blum up, throughout the six furlong event. Straightening out for the stretch, Blum and Student Lamp had a three length lead. The crowd was going wild, but Mister Market would not be shaken off. He kept coming and coming, closing the gap to two lengths, then one length, then a half length. Then Blum showed what he was all about. He had had the lead from the start, but he had saved enough horse so that in the stretch, when challenged, he could call upon his horse for a final charge. So when Mister Market drew up to within a half length of him, Blum went into a deep crouch, tapped the horse twice on the right, and drew off and away. Fittingly, he won his 4,000th race in the style that distinguished him.

In the winner's circle he stood in back of the sign that said "4,000" while Jim Raftery clicked away. He smiled broadly. There were cheers, and there were boos.

In the tunnel, watching Walter Blum pose for his pictures, were Pete Mikos and Humberto Gracia. Pete Mikos said with a smile, "When are you going to win 4,000 races, Humberto?"

Humberto Gracia said, "Do not worry."

The crowd went back to the *Daily Racing Form* to study the next race.